Keith M. Kilty
Virginia E. Richardson
Elizabeth A. Segal
Editors

Income Security and Public Assistance for Women and Children

Pre-publication REVIEWS, COMMENTARIES, EVALUATIONS . . .

T his timely book critically examines current and emerging AFDC and child welfare policies. It includes a rich selection of chapters that are historical, analytical, empirical, and personal. It also examines past child welfare practices and the implications of recent welfare legislation for women and children.

A distinctive feature of this book is its inclusion of the voices of welfare recipients. An upper-middle-class housewife who was plunged into poverty tells her story. Another author describes the voices of welfare mothers.

This volume is a welcome addition to the library of social work practitioners, educators, students, and any others who are concerned about the impact of poverty policies on women and children.

Roberta G. Sands, PhD
Associate Professor, University of Pennsylvania School of Social Work

The chapters are relevant, exciting and a powerful tool for demystifying and educating others about welfare reform. This book powerfully blends the historical facts and research on welfare with the personal life experiences of poor women and children. It also brings to light how legislation, the federal government, and welfare reform policies will be devastating to the truly oppressed–women who MUST take care of their children. It serves as an inspirational piece to hear in various forms the unheard voices of the millions of poor women and children who will suffer the most from welfare reform. This volume offers insights that will empower educators and social activists to counter those indifferent to the plights of the poor in the midst of welfare reform.

Carmen I. Aponte, PhD
Visiting Assistant Professor,
Dept. of Social Work SUNY College
at Brockport

This timely book examines the provocative issue of income security and public assistance in American society. Welfare reform as a policy issue is uniquely analyzed from a multi-dimensional framework inclusive of the social, political, and economic components. The book offers a refreshing, inclusive collection of articles written from a conceptual, narrative, and research-focused orientation. The eclectic approach in this edited collection of readings enhances the knowledge base of professionals, students, policymakers, practitioners, and consumers of public assistance.

David A. Ellenbrook, PhD
Associate Professor of Social Work &
Sociology, Castleton State College,
Castleton, Vermont

"The four articles taken together add unique information from perspectives not found in the mainstream political or research writings. It is evident that all four have similarities: they describe a welfare system, particularly AFDC, which does not and has not worked well; and they argue that the new policies will even more catastrophic for women and children. But beyond these similarities, the articles diverge to cover different elements of the current issue and its personal and damaging impact on women and children. . . .

[T]he appeal of the articles, as a collective, develops from four interwoven elements: 1) the authors are all women, some of whom write from a personalized perspective; 2) the conceptual approach is feminist and implicitly, if not explicitly, ties the personal to the political; 3) the methodology embraces the spectrum from quantitative to qualitative analysis, and from political to empirical to conceptual argument; 4) the suggestions for improvement are also broad, ranging from national policy (earned income tax credit) to state variations of TANF, to support groups and networks for women.

The language interspersed throughout these articles is connected not only to a rational core, but to an emotional and humanistic one as well: "to address the issue of income security for children with a nonwelfare, investment-oriented ideology and a strong national commitment to nurturing our nation's children"; a "feminist methodology which allows stories of otherwise silenced people to be heard"; and "a more human expansion of policy would allow women a choice."

Karen S. Haynes, PhD, MSW
President, University of Houston-Victoria

Income Security
and Public Assistance
for Women and Children

Income Security
and Public Assistance
for Women and Children

Keith M. Kilty
Virginia E. Richardson
Elizabeth A. Segal
Editors

The Haworth Press, Inc.
New York • London

Income Security and Public Assistance for Women and Children has also been published as *Journal of Poverty*, Volume 1, Number 2 1997.

The development, preparation, and publication of this work has been undertaken with great care. However, the publisher, employees, editors, and agents of The Haworth Press and all imprints of The Haworth Press, Inc., including The Haworth Medical Press and Pharmaceutical Products Press, are not responsible for any errors contained herein or for consequences that may ensue from use of materials or information contained in this work. Opinions expressed by the author(s) are not necessarily those of The Haworth Press, Inc.

Cover design by Donna Brooks

The Haworth Press, Inc., 10 Alice Street, Binghamton, NY 13904-1580 USA

Library of Congress Cataloging-in-Publication Data

Income security and public assistance for women and children / Keith M. Kilty, Virginia E. Richardson, Elizabeth A. Segal, editors.
    p. cm.
    Includes bibliographical references and index.
    ISBN 0-7890-0040-7 (alk. paper) – ISBN 0-7890-0047-4 (alk. paper)
    1. Aid to families with dependent children programs–United States. 2. Income maintenance programs–United States. 3. Welfare recipients–United States. 4. Poor children–United States. 5. Poor women–United States. 6. Women heads of households–United States. 7. Public welfare–United States. I. Kilty, Keith M. (Keith Michael), 1946- . II. Richardson, Virginia E. III. Segal, Elizabeth A.
HV699.I47 1997
362.71'0973–dc21
                                                 97-1462
                                                      CIP

INDEXING & ABSTRACTING

Contributions to this publication are selectively indexed or abstracted in print, electronic, online, or CD-ROM version(s) of the reference tools and information services listed below. This list is current as of the copyright date of this publication. See the end of this section for additional notes.

- *Abstracts in Social Gerontology: Current Literature on Aging,* National Council on the Aging, Library, 409 Third Street SW, 2nd Floor, Washington, DC 20024

- *Abstracts of Research in Pastoral Care & Counseling,* Loyola College, 7135 Minstrel Way, Suite 101, Columbia, MD 21045

- *Alzheimer's Disease Education & Referral Center (ADEAR),* Combined Health Information Database (CHID), P.O. Box 8250, Silver Spring, MD 20907-8250

- *Applied Social Sciences Index & Abstracts (ASSIA) (Online: ASSI via Data-Star) (CDRom: ASSIA Plus),* Bowker-Saur Limited, Maypole House, Maypole Road, East Grinstead, West Sussex RH19 1HH, England

- *caredata CD: the social and community care database,* National Institute for Social Work, 5 Tavistock Place, London WC1H 9SS, England

- *Central Library & Documentation Bureau,* International Labour Office, CH-1211 Geneva 22, Switzerland

- *CNPIEC Reference Guide: Chinese National Directory of Foreign Periodicals,* P.O. Box 88, Beijing, People's Republic of China

- *Criminal Justice Abstracts,* Willow Tree Press, 15 Washington Street, 4th Floor, Newark, NJ 07102

- *Family Studies Database (online and CD/ROM),* National Information Services Corporation, 306 East Baltimore Pike, 2nd Floor, Media, PA 19063

(continued)

- ***Guide to Social Science & Religion in Periodical Literature,*** National Periodical Library, P.O. Box 3278, Clearwater, FL 34630

- ***Health Management Information Service (HELMIS),*** Nuffield Institute for Health, 71-75 Clarendon Road, Leeds LS2 9PL, England

- ***Index to Periodical Articles Related to Law,*** University of Texas, 727 East 26th Street, Austin, TX 78705

- ***INTERNET ACCESS (& additional networks) Bulletin Board for Libraries ("BUBL"), coverage of information resources on INTERNET, JANET, and other networks.***
  - JANET X.29: UK.AC.BATH.BUBL or 00006012101300
  - TELNET: BUBL.BATH.AC.UK or 138.38.32.45 login 'bubl'
  - Gopher: BUBL.BATH.AC.UK (138.32.32.45). Port 7070
  - World Wide Web: http://www.bubl.bath.ac.uk./BUBL/home.html
  - NISSWAIS: telnetniss.ac.uk (for the NISS gateway)
  The Andersonian Library, Curran Building, 101 St. James Road, Glasgow G4 ONS, Scotland

- ***Mental Health Abstracts (online through DIALOG),*** IFI/Plenum Data Company, 3202 Kirkwood Highway, Wilmington, DE 19808

- ***National Library Database on Homelessness,*** National Coalition for the Homeless, 1612 K Street, NW, #1004, Homelessness Information Exchange, Washington, DC 20006

- ***Political Science Abstracts,*** IFI/Plenum Data Company, 3202 Kirkwood Highway, Wilmington, DE 19808

- ***Referativnyi Zhurnal,*** The Institute of Scientific Information, Baltijskaja ul., 14, Moscow, A-219, Republic of Russia

- ***Social Work Abstracts,*** National Association of Social Workers, 750 First Street NW, 8th Floor, Washington, DC 20002

- ***Sociological Abstracts (SA),*** Sociological Abstracts, Inc., P.O. Box 22206, San Diego, CA 92192-0206

(continued)

SPECIAL BIBLIOGRAPHIC NOTES

related to special journal issues (separates)
and indexing/abstracting

☐ indexing/abstracting services in this list will also cover material in any "separate" that is co-published simultaneously with Haworth's special thematic journal issue or DocuSerial. Indexing/abstracting usually covers material at the article/chapter level.

☐ monographic co-editions are intended for either non-subscribers or libraries which intend to purchase a second copy for their circulating collections.

☐ monographic co-editions are reported to all jobbers/wholesalers/approval plans. The source journal is listed as the "series" to assist the prevention of duplicate purchasing in the same manner utilized for books-in-series.

☐ to facilitate user/access services all indexing/abstracting services are encouraged to utilize the co-indexing entry note indicated at the bottom of the first page of each article/chapter/contribution.

☐ this is intended to assist a library user of any reference tool (whether print, electronic, online, or CD-ROM) to locate the monographic version if the library has purchased this version but not a subscription to the source journal.

☐ individual articles/chapters in any Haworth publication are also available through the Haworth Document Delivery Services (HDDS).

ABOUT THE EDITORS

Keith M. Kilty, PhD, is Professor in the College of Social Work at Ohio State University in Columbus. He has published or presented more than 50 papers and is an editorial reviewer for *ALCOHOLISM: Clinical and Experimental Research,* the *Journal of Studies on Alcohol,* and the *American Education Research Journal*, and Assistant Editor for the *Journal of Drug Issues.* Dr. Kilty is a member of the Society for the Study of Social Problems and a member of its Committee on Standards and Freedom of Research, Publication, and Teaching, and a member and Treasurer of the Bertha Capen Reynolds Society.

Virginia E. Richardson, PhD, MSW, is Professor in the College of Social Work at Ohio State University in Columbus where she is also Faculty Fellow in the Office of Geriatrics and Gerontology. An experienced clinical social worker, she has published over 40 papers and has presented at numerous workshops and conferences around the country. Dr. Richardson is a charter member of the Society for Social Work and Research, and a member of the National Association of Social Workers, the Gerontological Society of America, and the Council on Social Work Education.

Elizabeth A. Segal, PhD, MSW, is Associate Professor in the School of Social Work at Arizona State University in Tempe. She has made many presentations and conducted workshops and seminars on various issues concerning social work, and she is the author of many articles, book chapters, book reviews, proceedings, and reports. She served as a policy analyst in Washington, DC, as an American Association for the Advancement of Science Fellow. Dr. Segal is a member of the National Association of Social Workers, the Council on Social Work Education, and the Bertha Capen Reynolds Society.

Income Security and Public Assistance for Women and Children

CONTENTS

EDITORS' INTRODUCTION

A Legislative Update

The 1996 legislative year has witnessed a passion for welfare reform—by states and by Congress. Over the past couple of years, most states submitted requests for federal waivers to change their public assistance programs and in the process gain greater state control. The 104th Congress capped off the efforts in July 1996 by passing sweeping legislation that radically transformed the programs of federal aid to people who are poor. The attempts at change are not about the well-being of our nation nor are they about ways for government to help people. The legislative frenzy is about ending a relationship between government and people in need. After 61 years, the federal government will no longer guarantee financial support for poor women, children, elderly, and people with disabilities. What has been heralded as "welfare reform," a deceptively progressive sounding notion, is really the dismantling of the only national program designed

[Haworth co-indexing entry note]: "A Legislative Update." Kilty, Keith M., Virginia E. Richardson, and Elizabeth A. Segal. Co-published simultaneously in *Journal of Poverty* (The Haworth Press, Inc.) Vol. 1, No. 2, 1997, pp. 1-4; and: *Income Security and Public Assistance for Women and Children* (ed: Keith M. Kilty, Virginia E. Richardson, and Elizabeth A. Segal) The Haworth Press, Inc., 1997, pp. 1-4. Single or multiple copies of this article are available for a fee from The Haworth Document Delivery Service [1-800-342-9678, 9:00 a.m. - 5:00 p.m. (EST). E-mail address: getinfo@haworth.com].

1

specifically to assist poor women and children, the Aid to Families with Dependent Children program.

The AFDC program, originally passed as part of the 1935 Social Security Act, has for more than six decades served as the only cash assistance program for poor women and children. On average, it provides $381 dollars per month for the typical family of one female parent and her two children (Administration for Children and Families, 1995). In the realm of government expenses, it is small. AFDC consumes about one percent of the national budget (Budget of the United States Government, FY 1996, 1995). The defense budget is 18 times larger; the interest paid on the national debt is 13 times larger. As for social welfare dollars, the federal government spends 20 times more for social security checks than it does for AFDC checks. The reform efforts to save significant dollars on a program that overall does not command much of the budget is a fraud. The reality is that we have elected politicians who feel comfortable with dismantling the one and only financial support program for poor women and children.

When all the dust settles and we examine the consequences on AFDC of the 1996 Welfare Reform Act, we will find that the lives of the four million women and almost 10 million children, the majority of whom are under seven years of age (Administration for Children and Families, 1995), will have been significantly changed. Foremost in the legislation is the end to the federal guarantee that all qualified individuals will receive public assistance. States will receive a block grant, a set amount of dollars, to provide public assistance. When that runs out, there are no more federal moneys. States are free to set eligibility standards and decide who is worthy of receiving assistance. One of the key reasons the federal government took an active role in AFDC over the years is because states, left to their own, were reluctant and minimal in providing assistance. Returning complete control to state governments will see a return to the stringent eligibility rules and low benefits characteristic of state AFDC programs before stronger federal involvement.

The harshest components of the legislation will affect poor children severely. According to the legislation, within two years of receiving benefits, the head of every family must be working, otherwise the entire family will lose all benefits. No matter what happens in a woman's life, she will be eligible to receive no more than a lifetime total of five years worth of assistance. For her children, the same five-year cap applies. After that, the state will withdraw support ("Points of Agreement," 1996).

Furthermore, in six years, states must demonstrate a decrease in the number of AFDC recipients. While the rhetoric of politicians claims efforts to put people to work, there are no supports for employment training or job creation. In fact, in order for states to meet the requirement for a decrease in numbers of recipients, there is nothing stopping them from making eligibility more difficult. Instead of helping people to find jobs, state programs can cut people off of public assistance in order to meet the caseload reduction goals outlined within the Welfare Reform legislation of 1996 (Center for Law and Social Policy, 1996).

As policy analysts and social service providers we must ask ourselves: why this overwhelming national need to strip away the one safety net available to women and children? There are undoubtedly many possible reasons for this strong national sentiment: frustration with not "winning" the War on Poverty; intolerance for what appears to be a racial problem—although in reality AFDC serves women and children of *all* races; disdain for what appears to be the independence women "enjoy" by receiving monthly checks from the government; the sense of "I work hard for mine, why don't welfare recipients?"; or maybe the faulty assumption that this really will balance the budget.

Regardless of the underlying reasons driving the public and politicians, the end result will be catastrophic. While AFDC is not a perfect program, it is a last resort for women raising children who have no other means of adequate financial support. For many women who need AFDC, a five-year overall limit or a two-year increment limit may not affect them. But for many others, this mandated deadline will mean the disintegration of already fragile families. In a nation where it is increasingly harder and harder to raise children on one adult's income, particularly at the wages women are paid, it will become impossible for former AFDC recipients to do so. Struggling families will become homeless and women will find themselves fighting to keep their children.

Poor women are caught in a value bind–zealots for family values are fighting to keep women at home to raise children, while they are simultaneously dismantling the one program that allows poor women to do just that. The policy message is loud and clear–white, middle-class, *married* women should stay home, while poor, single, minority women should go out and work at any possible job, even if the wages paid are substandard to support a family. The inequity of this value contradiction becomes clear–at its base is racism, sexism, and classism.

So, today's welfare reform hits at all levels of inequality and demands our attention. This publication is dedicated to discussing the needs of poor women and children. These papers raise issues that preceded the new welfare reform, and suggest that the inequities and problems with the system will only worsen under the new legislation. We call your attention to the mix in this volume of academic discussions and personal experience. The degradation women who are poor face as they struggle to raise their families and the increasing loss of our children to poverty are presented in these papers. With the passage of this welfare reform legislation, the suffering and hardships will only increase. Our nation's clear lack of compassion at this point in history will serve as the foundation for our shame in the future. We must work to change these policy measures and to ensure that all families, regardless of race, class, or sex, have adequate income and support.

Keith M. Kilty
Virginia E. Richardson
Elizabeth A. Segal

REFERENCES

Administration for Children and Families. (1995). *Characteristics and financial circumstances of AFDC recipients FY 1993*. Washington, DC: US Government Printing Office.

Budget of the United States Government, fiscal year 1996. (1995). Washington, DC: US Government Printing Office.

Center for Law and Social Policy. (1996). *The welfare bill's work requirements*. Washington, DC: Author.

"Points of agreement, and disagreement, on the welfare bill." (1996, August 1). *The New York Times*, p. A8.

Federal Role
in Establishing National Income Security
for Children

Martha N. Ozawa

SUMMARY. As the United States attempts to minimize public spending on social welfare programs and to shift the authority over many programs to the states, the federal government needs to establish a program of income security for children that is not tied to welfare. Such a program is in the national interest because the country will need a strong, competent workforce to deal with stiffer global economic competition and a greater financial obligation to support the elderly. This article discusses why income security for children cannot be provided by the current system of income transfers and advocates the establishment of a $1,000 refundable tax credit for all children and an expansion of the Earned Income Tax Credit. *[Article copies available for a fee from The Haworth Document Delivery Service: 1-800-342-9678. E-mail address: getinfo@haworth.com]*

KEYWORDS. Federal role, children, income security, inter-state inequity, work incentives

The federal government is confronted with a great challenge: to cut expenditures for welfare programs and to invest more public resources in

---

Martha N. Ozawa, PhD, is Bettie Bofinger Brown Professor of Social Policy, George Warren Brown School of Social Work, Washington University, St. Louis, MO 63130-4899.

[Haworth co-indexing entry note]: "Federal Role in Establishing National Income Security for Children." Ozawa, Martha N. Co-published simultaneously in *Journal of Poverty* (The Haworth Press, Inc.) Vol. 1, No. 2, 1997, pp. 5-23; and: *Income Security and Public Assistance for Women and Children* (ed: Keith M. Kilty, Virginia E. Richardson, and Elizabeth A. Segal) The Haworth Press, Inc., 1997, pp. 5-23. Single or multiple copies of this article are available for a fee from The Haworth Document Delivery Service [1-800-342-9678, 9:00 a.m. - 5:00 p.m. (EST). E-mail address: getinfo@haworth.com].

the nation's children if the country is to have a future workforce with the skills necessary to compete in the global economy and to support the impending retirees of the baby-boom generation, each of whom will have to be supported by only two workers, instead of the current three (Board of Trustees, 1995). How the country can meet this challenge and the federal government's role in dealing with it are major issues.

The government's push to cut expenditures for welfare programs is in response to negative public attitudes toward welfare families, which are compounded by the fact that, increasingly, women are becoming dependent on welfare because they give birth out of wedlock as teenagers. In 1991, as many as 53% of the children on Aid to Families with Dependent Children (AFDC) had mothers who had never been married, compared with 32% in 1973 (U.S. House of Representatives, 1993, p. 696). Of the $47.27 billion that were spent for all AFDC families, through AFDC, Medicaid, and food stamps in 1990, an estimated $25.05 billion (or 52%) were spent for AFDC families whose dependence was the result of teenage pregnancy and child birth. The annual public expenditures to support each such family increased from $13,902 per year in 1985 to $28,123 per year in 1990, in 1990 dollars (U.S. House of Representatives, 1993, p. 1148).

Responding to the public's apprehension about welfare programs and their recipients, the Republican Party quickly proceeded to implement the Contract with America as soon as the party gained power in both houses of Congress. In an attempt to reform welfare, the Republican-led House of Representatives passed, on March 24, 1995, the Personal Responsibility Act (H.R. 4) and the Republican-led Senate passed, on September 20, 1995, the Work Opportunity Act (H.R. 4). Although some of the provisions of the two versions of H.R. 4 are different, blockgranting of AFDC (which will be called Block Grants for Temporary Assistance for Needy Families, TANF) and limiting its payments to two years per episode and five years during a woman's lifetime are likely to become part of the new law, thus ending the entitlement principal. The blockgranting of other programs, such as Medicaid, is also likely. States may be given the option of taking food stamps assistance as a block grant. Furthermore, Supplemental Security Income benefits will no longer be provided to substance abusers and to children whose disabilities do not meet the severity requirements in the Social Security Administration's medical listing of impairments (Burke, Richardson, Solomon, Spar, & Vialet, 1995).

American children have enormous problems. Nearly 20% of those aged 3-17 had, in 1988, at least one developmental, learning, or behavioral disorder (Zill & Schoenborn, 1990), and child abuse and neglect tripled between 1976 and 1986 (U.S. Bureau of the Census, 1990, p. 176). In addition, only one in seven eighth graders had a proficiency in math expected for that grade, and at age 17, half the high school students in this country could not handle decimals, fractions, and percentages to solve simple equations (Applebee, Langer, & Mullis, 1989; DeWitt, 1991). In 1988, American 13-year-old students scored the lowest in math and science tests compared to those from Ireland, Korea, Spain, and the United Kingdom (U.S. Department of Education, 1991, p. 1143). Furthermore, the U.S. rank in infant mortality declined from 13th in 1960 to 20th in 1988, and in 1990, the leading causes of death among 15 to 24 year olds were accidents, homicide, and suicide, in that order. In the face of the rapidly declining quality of life among children, the 1990 per capita social welfare expenditures for children were only one-eleventh of those for the elderly (U.S. House of Representatives, 1993, pp. 1165, 1179, 1564, and 1567).

The declining economic status of children compounds the deterioration of their living conditions. Fuchs and Reklis (1992) demonstrated that from 1960 to 1988, the median household income per child decreased from 67% to 63% of the median household income per adult aged 18-64 and from 84% to 68% of the median household income per elderly person. In the meantime, the official poverty rate of children surpassed that of elderly persons in 1974 and reached 21.9% in 1992, a rate 1.7 times as high as that of elderly persons (U.S. House of Representatives, 1994, p. 1158).

With this scenario as a backdrop, this article (1) explains why the current system of public transfers, particularly AFDC (or TANF as of 1996), cannot be a means through which public resources are channeled effectively to children and (2) advocates for the direct involvement of the federal government in establishing income security for children.

DEFICIENCIES IN THE CURRENT SYSTEM

The current system of public income transfers is inappropriate and incapable of providing income security for children for four reasons: (1) AFDC (or TANF) dilutes the attempt of other programs to improve work incentives, (2) the allocation of federal funds (or block grants) to finance AFDC (or TANF) is inherently inequitable and counterproductive, (3) the philosophical underpinning of AFDC (or TANF) is incompatible with the ideology of investment in children, and (4) public income transfers fail to provide an effective safety net for children.

AFDC's Adverse Effects on Work Incentives

Currently, AFDC reduces assistance payments dollar for dollar as AFDC families increase their earnings. Because of the high benefit-reduction rate, which diminishes the value of work to zero in dollar terms, it is difficult to enhance work incentives through other programs. Moreover, AFDC's objective of providing adequate benefits clashes with the goal of the Earned Income Tax Credit (EITC) to improve work incentives. Figures 1 and 2 depict the situations of three-member families (a mother and two

FIGURE 1. Effects of income transfers and taxes on net total family income, 1996 (in 1994 dollars): The case of families of three, New York City

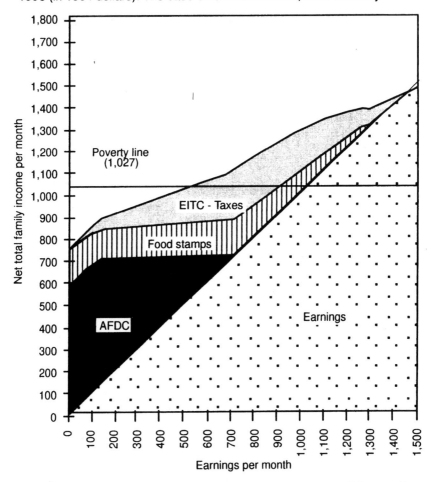

Source: Martha N. Ozawa, "The Earned Income Tax Credit: Its Effect and Its Significance," *Social Service Review, 69* (December 1995), p. 568, published by the University of Chicago Press. Used with permission.

FIGURE 2. Effects of income transfers and taxes on net total family income, 1996 (in 1994 dollars): The case of families of three, Texas

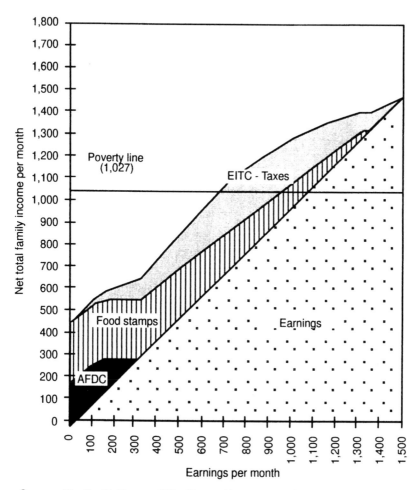

Source: Martha N. Ozawa, "The Earned Income Tax Credit: Its Effect and Its Significance," *Social Service Review, 69* (December 1995), p. 569, published by the University of Chicago Press. Used with permission.

children) in New York City and Texas who are on AFDC and are subjected to an EITC subsidy rate, the implicit tax rates in the AFDC and Food Stamp programs, and the explicit tax rates of the payroll tax and eventually of the federal income tax as the families' incomes increase. These figures illustrate what the financial situations of AFDC families might have been at various levels of earnings in 1994 if the EITC had been fully phased in as provided by the 1993 Omnibus Budget Reconciliation Act (OBRA).

It is clear from these figures that AFDC undermines the work incentive of the AFDC family in New York City, which provides generous payments, more than that of the AFDC family in Texas, which provides meager payments. The New York City family is subjected to cumulative implicit marginal tax rates ranging from 31.7% to 61.7%, except when its earnings are less than $120 a month, for which a positive subsidy of 8.4% applies. In contrast, the Texas family enjoys the positive subsidy of 8.4% for a wide range of earnings levels–from $1-$120 and $305-$702 a month; that is, within these ranges of earnings, each dollar earned brings the family a net income of $1.08.

Although the EITC improves the work incentives of the New York City family to a considerably lesser degree than of the Texas family, it enables the New York City family to escape poverty with greater ease. That is, with the EITC, the New York City family needs to work only 126 hours a month, or 73% of full-time work hours, but the Texas family has to work 151 hours a month, or 87% of full-time work hours, to achieve the same goal.

These examples indicate that the objective of providing adequate AFDC payments clashes with the intent of the EITC to enhance work incentives. This dilemma is keenly felt in New York City. Ironically, in states, such as Texas, that provide meager AFDC payments, the EITC is much more effective in increasing incentives for AFDC families to work. Thus, policymakers always face a trade-off between adequacy versus work incentives when they attempt to provide income support to low-income families through means-tested programs or a combination of such programs and a wage-subsidy program. If the United States wishes to provide adequate income security for children without compromising the work incentive, it will have to do so outside the welfare domain.

Inequitable Allocation of Block Grants

Since the inception of AFDC in 1935, the federal government has participated in funding the program only indirectly. Because the Social Security Act of 1935 left the level of AFDC payments up to the states, the federal government uses the grants-in-aid to help the states pay for AFDC on the basis of a matching formula, which is slanted in favor of poor states. Under the current formula, nominally called the Medicaid Matching Formula, the federal government subsidizes AFDC payments at rates ranging from 50% to 83%, depending on the per capita income of a state. However, because AFDC payments are so low in many poor states, the use of the apparently progressive formula does not necessarily translate into larger average subsidies per recipient in poor states. Moreover, because the AFDC payment levels are related to the percentage of African Americans in a state, the average federal subsidies per recipient have also inadvertently become related to race. A study by Ozawa (1991) found that states with low per capita incomes and states with a high percentage of African Americans receive smaller subsidies per recipient than do states with the opposite characteristics. Therefore, one can expect that the allocation of federal block grants for TANF, as prescribed in H.R. 4, which is also based on the Medicaid Matching Formula, will be related to per capita income and race in the same way.

Table 1 presents the 1996 allocation of federal block grants to states to finance TANF under H.R. 4 in two ways: (1) the average block grant per recipient and (2) the average block grant per poor person. The allocation is for 1996. As the table shows, the average federal block grant per poor person would vary among the states even more greatly than the average block grant per recipient. In 1996, New York would receive the highest block grant per recipient ($1,938.35) and Mississippi would receive the lowest ($477.75), with the median state, New Jersey, receiving $1,085.90. In terms of federal block grants per poor person, Alaska would receive the highest amount ($1,166.47) and Alabama would receive the lowest ($123.42), with the median state, Montana, receiving $361.79. These interstate variations would be far greater than the cost-of-living differences among the states.

Table 2 presents the results of a regression analysis of average federal block grants per recipient and per poor person. These two indicators of federal grants are regressed on the per capita income of a state and the percentage of African Americans in a state. All variables are transformed into natural logarithms.

As expected from earlier studies (Ozawa, 1991, 1995c), states with high per capita incomes would receive considerably larger federal block grants per recipient than would states with low per capita incomes ($t = 6.941; p < .0001$). The disparity in block grants per poor person between states with high and low per capita incomes would be just as great ($t = 7.417; p < .0001$). Translated into dollars, state A with a per capita income that would be $1,000 higher than that of state B would receive a federal block grant per recipient that is $91.72 larger. Similarly, state A would receive $70.81 more in federal block grants per poor person than would state B.

The amount of federal block grants per recipient that states would

TABLE 1. Average block grants for TANF, 1996

Per Recipient		Per Poor Person	
States	Amount ($)	States	Amount ($)
New York	1938.35	Alaska	1166.47
Alaska	1867.43	Dist. of Columbia	829.30
Hawaii	1723.23	New York	812.05
Vermont	1538.44	Massachusetts	756.71
Idaho	1499.07	Connecticut	745.11
California	1491.34	Rhode Island	728.18
Dist. of Columbia	1480.05	California	708.98
Connecticut	1429.17	Vermont	707.00
Rhode Island	1410.73	Washington	693.25
Massachusetts	1394.04	Hawaii	691.87
Washington	1388.92	Michigan	606.82
Oregon	1382.37	Wisconsin	561.26
Minnesota	1334.13	Ohio	505.08
Utah	1324.85	New Jersey	496.87
New Mexico	1308.91	Oregon	470.94
New Hampshire	1297.77	Minnesota	465.26
Wisconsin	1276.82	Delaware	460.11
Montana	1251.02	Maine	445.56
North Dakota	1245.58	Wyoming	432.04
Iowa	1210.17	Utah	427.49
Kansas	1161.13	Pennsylvania	417.85
Michigan	1131.26	Maryland	383.12
Arizona	1127.97	Iowa	378.51
Maine	1120.94	Arizona	376.76
Wyoming	1115.74	New Hampshire	375.65
New Jersey	1085.90	Montana	361.79
Oklahoma	1049.11	New Mexico	360.05
South Dakota	1019.95	Kansas	357.65
Nebraska	1008.00	Colorado	332.89
Pennsylvania	997.05	North Dakota	315.64
Indiana	997.02	Indiana	304.53
Nevada	989.76	Illinois	290.72
Maryland	982.53	Nebraska	288.46
Colorado	954.68	Georgia	273.87
Delaware	940.04	West Virginia	270.41
Ohio	936.70	North Carolina	266.61
West Virginia	900.54	Virginia	263.42
North Carolina	871.11	Missouri	258.03
Florida	824.38	Florida	253.03
Missouri	811.49	Kentucky	243.43
Virginia	806.09	Oklahoma	239.76
Georgia	802.12	Tennessee	198.69
Illinois	779.91	South Dakota	197.64
Kentucky	767.19	Idaho	187.26

Per Recipient		Per Poor Person	
States	Amount ($)	States	Amount ($)
Arkansas	739.13	Nevada	173.73
South Carolina	686.95	Louisiana	150.56
Alabama	621.81	Texas	142.90
Tennessee	609.14	South Carolina	141.17
Texas	574.34	Arkansas	130.05
Louisiana	565.40	Mississippi	127.77
Mississippi	477.75	Alabama	123.42

Source: Derived from Gene Falk, "Preliminary Comparison of House- and Senate-Passed H.R. 4 Financing Provisions for Temporary Assistance and Child Care," *Memorandum,* Congressional Research Service, October 12, 1995; Social Security Administration, *Annual Statistical Supplement, 1994, to Social Security Bulletin* (Washington, DC: Author, 1994), Table 9G, p. 344; U.S. Bureau of the Census, *Statistical Abstract of the United States, 1994* (114th ed.) (Washington, DC: U.S. Government Printing Office, 1994), Table 732, p. 477.

TABLE 2. Regression analysis of TANF per recipient and TANF per poor person, 1996

	TANF per Recipient		TANF per Poor Person	
	Coefficient	t value	Coefficient	t value
Intercept	−5.532	−3.029*	−20.340	−5.726***
Per capita income	1.317	6.941***	2.737	7.417***
Percentage of African Americans	−0.143	−7.399***	−0.144	−3.816**
N	51		51	
R^2	0.637		0.555	
F	42.152***		29.986***	

* $p < .01$; ** $p < .001$; *** $p < .0001$.

Source: Gene Falk, "Preliminary Comparison of House- and Senate-Passed H.R. 4 Financing Provisions for Temporary Assistance and Child Care," *Memorandum,* Congressional Research Service, October 12, 1995; Social Security Administration, *Annual Statistical Supplement, 1994, to Social Security Bulletin* (Washington, DC: Author, 1994), Table 9G, p. 344; U.S. Bureau of the Census, *Statistical Abstract of the United States, 1994* (114th ed.) (Washington, DC: U.S. Government Printing Office, 1994), Table 732, p. 477.

receive is inversely related to the percentage of African Americans in the states. Federal block grants per recipient would be considerably larger in the states with a low percentage of African Americans than in the states with a high percentage ($t = -7.399$; $p < .0001$). The percentage of African Americans would exert a slightly less—but still powerful—effect on federal block grants per poor person ($t = -3.816$; $p < .0004$). In dollar terms, state A, with a proportion of African Americans that is 10 percentage points higher than that of state B, would receive $147.31 less in federal block grants per recipient. Likewise, state A would receive $54.89 less in block grants per poor person than would state B.

These regression results indicate that the allocation formula of H.R. 4 is inherently inequitable. The formula will result in smaller federal block grants for states with less economic capability and for states with a high percentage of African Americans, whether the block grants are per recipient or per poor person.

The Senate version of H.R. 4 attempts to rectify the inequitable allocation of federal funds. In particular, after 1996, a state would automatically qualify for an annual 2.5% increase in its grant if

1. its grant per poor person is less than 35% of the national average grant per poor person or
2. its population growth from April 1, 1990, to July 1, 1994, exceeded 10% (Falk, 1995).

The House version of H.R. 4 simply distributes $100 million annually to states according to the growth in their populations from 1997 through 2000.

The adjustment in the allocation of federal block grants on the basis of the 1996 TANF payment levels (the trigger point is 35% lower than the national average), as prescribed by the Senate version of H.R. 4, would hardly make a dent in the great disparity among states that would exist in 1996. According to calculations by the author, it would take 33 years for the federal block grant per recipient for Mississippi to catch up with the block grant for the median state if the block grant for Mississippi is allowed to grow at the compounded rate of 2.5%, as prescribed by the Senate version. Likewise, it would take 44 years for the federal block grant per poor person for Alabama to reach the block grant for the median state. Moreover, adjusting the federal block grants according to the growth in population would not, by definition, change the interstate variation in block grants.

The interstate variation in AFDC payments (and then in TANF in 1996 and thereafter) is a product of past social policies in the states, which were antithetical to the public interest in investing in all children wherever they live. Thus, AFDC and TANF cannot possibly be the foundation for providing income security for all American children.

Absence of an Investment Ideology

Although at its inception in 1935, AFDC was a benevolent program designed to help widows raise their children, over time it has become an unpopular program. The increasing hostility toward AFDC stems from the fact that since Survivors Insurance became a viable program to support families with widowed mothers, and the rates of divorce and out-of-wedlock births have increased, most AFDC families are headed by never-married or divorced mothers. These attitudes toward AFDC have been compounded by the new expectation that welfare mothers should work, as other mothers do.

The requirement that AFDC mothers must work was first incorporated into the Work Incentive Program in 1967. The 1981 OBRA made this requirement more explicit. The Job Opportunities and Skills Training program—the centerpiece of the 1988 Family Support Act—capitalized on the experiences gained from the 1981 OBRA. Its goal was to have 20% of nonexempt AFDC mothers participate by 1995; however, this goal was not achieved primarily because of the lack of state funds to match federal funds (U.S. House of Representatives, 1994, p. 356).

Wisconsin took the work requirement a step further. Under a federal waiver, Tommy Thompson, governor of Wisconsin, signed Act 99 into law on December 13, 1993. Termed Work Not Welfare, the Wisconsin program requires AFDC mothers to start working for AFDC benefits one year after they enroll in AFDC, and it terminates benefits one year later. The act also mandates the elimination of AFDC by 1999 (Ozawa, 1994).

In the meantime, numerous states started welfare reform programs under the federal waiver, many of which include punitive sanctions. For example, California pays no more to new residents than the benefit level of their previous state of residence for one year, New Jersey does not pay benefits to babies born to mothers while on AFDC, Wisconsin reduces the benefit increase for a new baby, Maryland reduces benefits by $25 per month per child if families fail to follow a prescribed schedule of health care services, and Missouri terminates eligibility for AFDC when AFDC children fail to attend school at least 80% of the school year (Burke, 1993).

Thus, the AFDC program has long ceased to be an income support program for children. Instead, it has become a program to train AFDC mothers and to move them into the labor force—with punitive sanctions, if necessary. For the first time, the federal government is sending a message that children born to certain mothers are unwelcome. What is worse, children have become a political pawn to control the behavior of low-income women who resort to welfare. In the political environment surrounding welfare, TANF will be an unsuitable program—both politically and practically—for investing in children.

Ineffectiveness of Income Transfers

In spite of the sizable amount of public spending on cash income transfers, which now approaches 9% of the gross national product (Bixby, 1994; U.S. Bureau of the Census, 1994, p. 446; U.S. Congressional Budget Office, 1995, p. 22), the system of public income transfers is incapable of providing an effective safety net for the nation's children. Table 3 presents the results of a study by Ozawa and Lum (1995), which found that after receiving social insurance benefits (unemployment and social security benefits) and welfare payments (all income-tested cash transfers, plus food stamps), the nation's poor children live, on average, at 66% of the poverty line, whereas elderly poor persons live at 76% of the poverty line. Note that although the economic status of poor children is much lower than many policymakers may wish to tolerate, it is welfare payments that are largely responsible for increasing the level of children's pretransfer income (32% of the poverty line) to the level of their posttransfer income (66% of the poverty line). For the elderly, it is largely social insurance benefits that lift their pretransfer income level (9% of the poverty line) to the posttransfer income level (76% of the poverty line).

(A separate data analysis of the same data set used for the study by Ozawa and Lum, 1995, shows that among the three age groups of persons—children, adults, and elderly persons—the economic condition of children is the worst. The poverty ratio for all children is 2.56, compared with 3.06 for all elderly persons and 3.66 for all adults.)

A major reason why American children fare so poorly in improving their posttransfer income status, compared with those in other industrialized countries, is that the United States does not have income support

TABLE 3. Effects of public income transfers on poverty ratios of poor children, adults, and elderly persons, 1991

Measure	Pretransfer Income	Plus Social Insurance Benefits*	Plus Welfare Payments**	% Change Due to All
Poverty ratios				
Children	0.32	0.37	0.66	
Adults	0.32	0.40	0.60	
Elderly persons	0.09	0.64	0.76	
Percentage change				
Children		16	91	106
Adults		25	63	88
Elderly persons		611	133	744

*   Includes social security and unemployment benefits.
** Includes all means-tested cash payments and food stamps.

Source: Martha N. Ozawa and Yat-sang Lum, "How Safe is the Safety Net for Poor Children." Unpublished manuscript, Washington University, St. Louis.

programs specifically targeted to children—notably children's allowance and child support assurance (Rainwater & Smeeding, 1995). In the United States, transfer programs that involve large public expenditures do not affect the economic condition of most children. For example, as is clear from Table 3, the social security and unemployment insurance programs, for which the United States spent as much as $301 billion in 1991 (Bixby, 1994, p. 99), contribute little toward improving the income status of poor children. In addition, welfare programs in which many poor children participate involve relatively small expenditures and, thus, cannot effectively improve the economic status of children (Ozawa, 1995a).

The inappropriateness of AFDC (and TANF from 1996) and the inability of the current system of income transfers to provide an effective safety net for children should lead the concerned policymakers to look for alternative approaches to establishing public policy on income security for children.

FEDERAL ROLE IN ESTABLISHING INCOME SECURITY FOR CHILDREN

By now, it is clear that it is in the national interest for the federal government to play an important role in establishing income security measures for children, so that future generations of workers can be equipped to deal with the dual challenge that this country faces: ensuring its economic growth and financially supporting the growing elderly population. Thus, the future generations of American children must have sufficient cognitive capabilities and physical strength, the levels of which should not vary according to the racial, ethnic, and economic backgrounds of their parents as much as they do now. To meet this challenge, the federal government must establish income security for children independently of the current congressional initiatives to transfer the authority over many welfare programs to state governments.

There are strategic reasons for establishing such a policy as well. First, because the demographic composition of states varies considerably, letting the states establish their own income security measures for children creates unequal burdens on the states. For example, states with large proportions of households with children will find it difficult to levy taxes on the rest of the households in them. Thus, the horizontal redistribution of income from childless households to those with children can be implemented most effectively only if income is redistributed nationwide. Second, the nationwide redistribution of income from childless households to those with children can bring about the vertical redistribution of income from the rich to the poor states. Third, the national government alone has the power to collect enough revenues to ensure a national minimum income for all children.

National Income Security for Children

A combination of a $1,000 refundable tax credit for all children and the EITC, as provided by the 1993 OBRA, can constitute this national income security. When the EITC is fully phased in in 1996, income security for a child who lives in a two-person family (one parent and a child) with a head who works fulltime at the minimum wage will be $3,156 ($2,156 from the EITC and $1,000 from the refundable tax credit). Likewise, the income security for each child who lives in a three-person family (one parent and two children) with a head who works fulltime at the minimum wage will be $2,782 ($1,782 from the EITC plus $1,000 from the refundable tax credit). Similarly, the income security for each child who lives in a four-person family (one parent and three children) with a head who works fulltime at the minimum wage will be $2,188 ($1,188 from the EITC and $1,000 from the refundable tax credit) (Ozawa, 1995b).

If annual earnings at the minimum wage ($8,823 = $4.25 × 2,076 hours of work) are added to national income security for children, the income of a two-member family with one child will be $11,979 (113% of the poverty line); of a three-member family with two children, $14,387 (114% of the poverty line); of a four-member family with three children, $15,387 (95% of the poverty line) (Social Security Administration, 1994, p. 151).[1]

These calculations indicate that even a single-parent family with one or two children can escape poverty as long as the parent works fulltime at the minimum wage. Put differently, as long as the head of the family can meet his or her own economic needs through work (the poverty line for a family of one in 1996 is estimated to be $8,212 [Social Security Administration, 1994, p. 151]), the family's income will be above the poverty line because the children will bring their own economic resources to the family through the national income security measures outlined here.

The amount of EITC, provided under the 1993 OBRA, is the same for families with two or more children, assuming that the earned income is the same. Thus, children in large families will be provided for less adequately. The example just shown indicates that families with three–or more–children whose head works fulltime at the minimum wage will live below the poverty line. However, in 1993 only 9% of families had three or more children, and only 2% of families had four or more children (U.S. Bureau of the Census, 1994, p. 64). Thus, if the federal government creates another bracket–families with three or more children–and provides the

EITC at a higher rate than for families with two children, the EITC will meet the economic needs of the vast majority of families with children. The unmet needs of the rest of large families can be dealt with through residual programs.

As illustrated, national income security for children can become a reality if the federal government (1) adopts the refundable tax credit of $1,000 for all children, as recommended by the National Commission on Children (National Commission on Children, 1991), and (2) improves the EITC provision, as provided under the 1993 OBRA, by introducing another bracket for families with three or more children.

Income security for children would have no adverse effect on the work incentives on heads of households who work at the minimum wage. The $1,000 refundable tax credit would be provided to all children, regardless of their parents' work status or the amount of their earnings. Furthermore, in 1996, the EITC will subsidize earned income at a stipulated rate until the annual earnings reach $8,910, in the case of a working head with two children, and $6,340 in the case of a working head with one child, thus providing positive work incentives for workers whose earnings are below these levels. Beyond these levels, the EITC stays the same (the maximum EITC) until the earnings reach $11,630 in both cases, thus creating no adverse effects on work incentives. Beyond the $11,630 level, the EITC begins to phase out, creating work disincentives. Thus, for a minimum wage worker, whose annual earnings are below $11,630, the EITC does not create negative work incentives.

Income security for children will minimize the role of AFDC (or TANF after 1996). As a result, the United States can address the issue of income security for children with a nonwelfare, investment-oriented ideology and a strong national commitment to nurturing the nation's children. At the same time, freed from a concern for providing income support for children, each state government can concentrate on the administration of its residual income support program, job training program, and social service program to assist low-income families using the standards and approaches that are compatible with the norms and aspirations of the people in the state.

Income security for children seems realistic for the United States to adopt. However, obstacles abound. The Republican-led Senate and House are proposing several measures to scale back the scope of the EITC. Pertinent to this article is the attempt to freeze the EITC provisions at the 1995 levels, instead of entirely phasing in these provisions as provided by the 1993 OBRA. In particular, the proposal would freeze the credit rate for families with two or more children at 36%, instead of increasing it to 40%

in 1996. In addition, the Senate proposal would increase the amount of the EITC that would be reduced from the current 15.89 cents to 18 cents for each dollar earned beyond $11,630, in the case of families with one child, and from 21.06 cents to 23 cents for each dollar earned beyond $11,630, in the case of families with two or more children. The House's proposal is even worse; it would increase the amount of the EITC that would be reduced to 23 cents for each dollar earned and to 28 cents for each dollar earned in these two situations, respectively (Storey, 1995). If these proposals are adopted, then the income of families with children (a combination of earnings, the EITC, and the refundable tax credit), would be lower than the examples discussed earlier.

The $1,000 refundable tax credit for children also faces obstacles on two fronts. First the recommended amount, $1,000, is twice the amount included in the Republican proposal (Calmes, 1995). Second, the refundability of the tax credit may face political opposition. The public may argue that the tax credit is for taxpayers to get back some of the taxes they have already paid, so they can use their "own" money for their children, and thus that nontaxpaying families have no right to receive such a credit.

Income security for children needs to be part of the political debate. Will the public support the scope of the EITC, as envisioned in the 1993 OBRA, so working families with children can have more adequate incomes than wages alone can provide? Will the public support a further expansion of the EITC by introducing another bracket for families with three or more children? Is the public ready to double the amount of tax credit for children and make the credit refundable, so the credit goes to all children, regardless of the taxpaying status of their parents?

CONCLUSIONS

As the United States shifts the authority over many social welfare programs from the federal government to the state governments, certain social welfare programs should stay under the federal government's authority. Income security for children is one of them. As this country takes on the rest of the world as both economic partners and competitors, it will be in the national interest to make sure that as many children as possible have human capital that is good enough to have high-paying jobs when they reach adulthood. Otherwise, future generations of workers will be unable to support the retired population adequately.

If the states developed their own income security programs for children, there would be interstate variations in provisions, as has occurred with other state-developed programs, such as unemployment insurance. A federally developed income security program for children would ensure that even children in the poorest state would have a minimum level of economic well-being, below which no child could fall.

Because income security for children is directly linked to the future of the American economy and the future of income support for the elderly, the program should be pursued outside the domain of welfare. Both philosophically and programmatically, welfare programs are unsuitable for establishing income security for children. The most appropriate way is to use the federal income tax system to collect revenues nationwide and to redistribute fiscal resources to children.

Establishing a national minimum income for children should be considered part of the national strategy for developing skills that are diverse in nature, but high and homogeneous in standards. In the final analysis, how well Americans can perform the tasks at hand will be the paramount issue, whatever types of occupations they may choose in the future. This point cannot be overemphasized because the major challenge the United States faces is whether it can create, in its racially, ethnically, and culturally diverse society, future generations of workers, out of the current generations of children, who will have a homogeneously high level of human capabilities.

NOTE

1. The projected 1996 figures for EITC were obtained from James R. Storey of Congressional Research Service, The Library of Congress, on Novermber 9, 1995. To calculate the 1996 poverty line, I inflated the 1993 figures at the compounded rate of 3 percent a year.

REFERENCES

Applebee, A.N., Langer, J.A., & Mullis, I.V.S. (1989). *Crossroads in American education*. Princeton, NJ: Educational Testing Service.

Bixby, A.K. (1994). Public social welfare expenditures, fiscal year 1991. *Social Security Bulletin*, 57(1):96-101.

Board of Trustees. (1995). *The 1995 annual report of the federal Old-Age and Survivors Insurance and Disability Insurance Trust Funds*. Washington, DC: U.S. Government Printing Office.

Burke, V. (1993). Time-limited welfare proposals. *CRS Issue Brief* (IB93034). Washington, DC: Congressional Research Service.

Burke, V., Richardson, J., Solomon, C., Spar, K., & Vialet, J. (1995). Welfare reform: The Senate-passed bill (H.R. 4). *CRS Report for Congress* (95-991 EPW). Washington, DC: Congressional Research Service.

Calmes, J. (1995, February 6). House GOP clears the way for passage of ambitious tax-reduction package. *Wall Street Journal*, p. 3.

DeWitt, K. (1991, June 7). Eighth graders' math survey shows no state of 'cutting it.' *New York Times*, p. 1.

Falk, G. (1995, October 2). Preliminary comparison of House- and Senate-passed H.R. 4 financing provisions for temporary assistance and child care. *Memorandum*. Washington, DC: Congressional Research Service.

Fuchs, V.R., & Reklis, D.M. (1992, January). American's children: Economic perspectives and policy options. *Science, 255*:41-46.

National Commission on Children. (1991). *Beyond rhetoric: A new American agenda for children and families*. Washington, DC: Author.

Ozawa, M.N. (1991). Unequal treatment of AFDC children by the federal government. *Children and Youth Services Review*, 13(4):257-269.

Ozawa, M.N. (1994). Women, children, and welfare reform. *Affilia: Women and Social Work*, 9:338-359.

Ozawa, M.N. (1995a.) Public spending on income-tested social welfare programs for investment and consumption purposes. *Journal of Sociology and Social Welfare*, 22(4): 132-146.

Ozawa, M.N. (1995b). The earned income tax credit: Its effects and its significance. *Social Service Review*, 69(4): 563-582.

Ozawa, M.N. (1995c). Medicaid matching formula, federal subsidies, and Medicaid payments. *Social Work Research*, 19(2):89-100.

Ozawa, M.N., & Lum, Y.S. (1995). How safe is the safety net for children? Unpublished manuscript. Washington University, St. Louis.

Rainwater, L., & Smeeding, T.M. (1995). Doing poorly: The real income of American children in a comparative perspective. Unpublished manuscript. Maxwell School of Citizenship and Public Affairs, Syracuse University, Syracuse, NY.

Social Security Administration. (1994). *Annual statistical supplement, 1994, to Social Security Bulletin*. Washington, DC: Author.

Storey, J.R. (1995). The earned income tax credit: Legislative issues in the 104th Congress, 1995. *CRS Report for Congress* (95-340 EPW). Washington, DC: Congressional Research Service.

U.S. Bureau of the Census. (1990). *Statistical abstract of the United States, 1990* (110th ed.). Washington, DC: U.S. Government Printing Office.

U.S. Bureau of the Census. (1994). *Statistical abstract of the United States: 1994* (114th ed.). Washington, DC: U.S. Government Printing Office.

U.S. Congressional Budget Office. (1995). *The economic and budget outlook: Update*. Washington, DC: U.S. Government Printing Office.

U.S. Department of Education, National Education Goals Panel. (1991). *The national education goals report: Building a nation of learners*. Washington, DC: U.S. Government Printing Office.

U.S. House of Representatives, Committee on Ways and Means. (1993). *Overview of entitlement programs: 1993 green book*. Washington, DC: U.S. Government Printing Office.

U.S. House of Representatives, Committee on Ways and Means. (1994). *Overview of entitlement programs: 1994 green book.* Washington, DC: U.S. Government Printing Office.

Zill, N., & Schoenborn, C.A. (1990). Developmental, learning, and emotional problems: Health of our nation's children, United States, 1988. *Advance Data* (No. 190). Washington, DC: U.S. Department of Health and Human Services.

Welfare Mothers Speak: One State's Effort to Bring Recipient Voices to the Welfare Debate

Sandra Sue Butler
Mary Katherine Nevin

SUMMARY. Recipients of AFDC are rarely asked what they think about welfare reform. As part of a multifaceted research effort designed to move the welfare debate in the state of Maine beyond myths and stereotypes, a coalition of activists, service providers and academics

Sandra Sue Butler, MSW, PhD, is Assistant Professor, School of Social Work, University of Maine, 5770 Annex C, Orono, ME 04469-5770 (E-mail: SBUTLER@ Maine.Maine.edu).

Mary Katherine Nevin is an MSW candidate at the School of Social Work, University of Maine.

The authors would like to thank members of the Women's Economic Security Project and the Women's Development Institute for their tireless efforts and for allowing access to their data. In particular Laura Fortman, Chris Hastedt, Mary Henderson, Stephanie Seguino and Linda Wilcox have offered invaluable assistance and enthusiasm. Primary gratitude is reserved for the 929 AFDC recipients who trusted the researchers enough to take the time to tell their stories and to offer their suggestions for welfare reform.

This research was funded by a Summer Research Faculty Grant from the University of Maine, and a version of this paper was presented in September, 1995, at the Annual Workshop of the National Association for Welfare Research and Statistics in Jackson Hole, Wyoming.

[Haworth co-indexing entry note]: "Welfare Mothers Speak: One State's Effort to Bring Recipient Voices to the Welfare Debate." Butler, Sandra Sue, and Mary Katherine Nevin. Co-published simultaneously in *Journal of Poverty* (The Haworth Press, Inc.) Vol. 1, No. 2, 1997, pp. 25-61; and: *Income Security and Public Assistance for Women and Children* (ed: Keith M. Kilty, Virginia E. Richardson, and Elizabeth A. Segal) The Haworth Press, Inc., 1997, pp. 25-61. Single or multiple copies of this article are available for a fee from The Haworth Document Delivery Service [1-800-342-9678, 9:00 a.m. - 5:00 p.m. (EST). E-mail address: getinfo@haworth.com].

25

created the AFDC Parent Survey and disseminated it to a random sample of AFDC families (n = 929). This article presents a thematic analysis of the narrative data resulting from the three open-ended questions on this survey which asked respondents what they needed in order to become economically self-sufficient. Six conceptual themes emerged from the data: struggling against odds; children are priority; catch-22; give us a chance; division of the oppressed; and thank you for listening. These six themes are presented through direct quotes from the respondents and implications of this research are discussed. *[Article copies available for a fee from The Haworth Document Delivery Service: 1-800-342-9678. E-mail address: getinfo@haworth.com]*

KEYWORDS. Welfare, poverty, feminist methodology, qualitative research, AFDC

INTRODUCTION

The public debate around welfare reform has become increasingly mean-spirited in the last decade of this century. The debate is based on negative myths and stereotypes of poor women which are not based on research and emphasize behavioral theories of poverty over structural and human capital explanations (Abramovitz, 1994; Rank, 1994). Abramovitz (1994) lists three reasons why the thrust of most current welfare reform is troublesome:

> First, women are the target of increasingly coercive measures. Second, these measures are gaining support based upon an appeal to misogynist and racist stereotypes of poor women and welfare. Third, women are being scapegoated by those who blame poverty on individual choices rather than on market forces. . . . (p. 17)

Since the mid-1980s individual states have been encouraged by the federal government to apply for waivers in order to experiment with different models of welfare reform. Before that time requests for waivers were rarely approved, and when they were it was generally for incremental policy changes or short-term demonstration projects (Thomas, 1995). Most of the resulting proposals have been punitive, penalizing women for a variety of circumstances, including: having more children while on welfare ("family cap"); failing to have a child immunized; failing to marry ("wedfare"); having children with poor school attendance ("learnfare"); and moving to a new state (Jones, 1995). These reforms have not been research supported and have succeeded only in humiliating and punishing families, not in assisting poor families to become self-supporting (Albelda & Tilly, 1994; Jones, 1995).

Coercive measures such as forcing women to work for their benefits (workfare) and imposing time limits on the length of time a family can receive Aid to Families with Dependent Children (AFDC) have also garnered considerable support recently from both Democrats and Republicans. If women's status in the labor market is not changed, current proposed reforms–such as time limits–will succeed only in disrupting the lives of millions of poor women and children, and could well have catastrophic consequences (Amott, 1994). Welfare reform which focuses on individual behaviors of welfare recipients and their children rather than on market barriers is doomed to fail. In short, there are not enough jobs available that pay livable wages–including health care and child care costs–for all the low-skilled women who currently receive AFDC.

While the idea of forcing women to work has considerable appeal in a society which values a strong work ethic, it does not take into account the realities of today's labor market. Cloward (1994) submits that workfare is a hoax and that welfare recipients are being scapegoated in order to draw attention away from economic malaise:

> Day after day, we pick up a newspaper and its big stories are about so-called welfare fraud and not about the income distribution fraud or the wealth concentration fraud. This is a period in which a great deal of emphasis has been placed on workfare. Yet it is increasingly clear that this is not a labor market that needs more unskilled workers. This is not a labor market that is prepared to pay people a living wage or one that is prepared to pay people decent benefits. (p. 39)

In 1988, The Family Support Act (FSA) was passed. This piece of legislation was heralded as constituting a new social contract between government and welfare recipients (Hagen & Lurie, 1995). As quoted in Hagen and Lurie (1995), Senator Moynihan, the chief architect of the legislation, noted: "In the act, Congress laid down a set of mutual obligations. Society owed single mothers support while they acquired the means to self-sufficiency; mothers owed the society the effort to become self-sufficient" (p. 523). In fact, though it authorized state welfare-to-work initiatives through the Job Opportunities and Basic Skills Training program (JOBS), this act was not a radical departure from previous AFDC legislation (Hagen & Lurie, 1995). In the seven years since the enactment of the FSA, politicians and the public are restless; the self-sufficiency supporters of the FSA predicted has not happened quickly enough for a society which looks for quick fixes to complicated problems.

Many believe the JOBS program was never given a chance. Without adequate funding it could never be fully implemented. Evaluation research of the JOBS program demonstrates that the program does have the potential for providing new opportunities for women to obtain education and training to compete for meaningful jobs in the labor market (Hagen, 1994); this outcome can only be attained through a much more generous commitment of resources than has happened to date. As stated by Hagen and Lurie (1995), ". . . the issue facing JOBS programs is not finding people to participate; it is finding the resources to allow them to receive education and training" (p. 531).

By the early 1990s, candidate–and, eventually, President–Clinton was talking about ending "welfare as we know it." To his credit, President Clinton recognized the need for access to health care, child care and jobs that pay enough–largely through the Earned Income Tax Credit–to make leaving welfare an attractive option. With the failure of the Administration's comprehensive health care reform, what remained of Clinton's welfare reform initiative was a focus on time limits and workfare. This opened the door for the new Republican Congress of 1994 to move welfare reform even further to the right. As part of the Republicans' Contract with America, the Personal Responsibility Act (PRA) was passed by the House of Representatives in March, 1994. This bill includes dramatic funding reductions–including converting the AFDC program into a block grant with fixed funding–and fundamental programmatic changes in many areas. These programmatic changes are similar to state initiatives which focus on individual behavior; examples of the groups to whom the PRA would prohibit cash assistance include: unmarried mothers under 18; any family who has received assistance for five years; and most legal immigrants. This bill would repeal the JOBS program and provide no new resources for states to continue their efforts to help people to earn their way off welfare (Parrott, 1995).

At the time of this writing, a welfare bill sponsored by Senator Dole has just passed in the Senate. This bill is slightly less harsh than its companion bill in the House though it also contains a five year time limit and converts AFDC from an entitlement to a block grant. The compromise bill that will result from Conference Committee negotiations will almost assuredly include time limits and the loss of entitlement status for AFDC. If President Clinton signs the compromise bill–as it is expected he will unless the House refuses to compromise–states will have far greater responsibility for designing their own welfare policies and programs.

THE CREATION OF THE AFDC SURVEY
AND THE RESULTING NARRATIVE DATA

For the past 15 years, a group of dedicated activists in Maine has worked to influence legislation affecting the lives of AFDC recipients. In particular, this group has advocated for the implementation of enriched education and training programs which allow AFDC participants to obtain adequate skills to qualify for jobs that pay a living wage. In addition, this group has fought at first to increase basic financial grants, and more recently to prevent cuts in these benefits. The lobbying and grass roots organizing efforts of these activists–primarily women–resulted, during a more progressive political environment in the early 1980s, in some relatively innovative training programs, and during more mean-spirited times, prevented draconian cuts in services and benefits.

In response to the punitive welfare reform bills being introduced in the state legislature and similar victim-blaming proposals at the federal level, a coalition of practitioner advocacy groups under the auspices of a nonprofit organization, the Women's Development Institute, formed in March, 1994 to collect objective information about the status of Maine families on AFDC. There existed a parallel effort involving the religious community, low-income advocates, women's organizations, and Community Action Programs which resulted in the formation of the Coalition for Economic Justice. This group took on public education about welfare reform as its major activity. A working committee on welfare reform began to meet regularly in order to proactively shift the terms of the welfare debate from one that focused on individual deficiencies to one that directed attention to the structural constraints encountered by women. This committee–later named the Women's Economic Security Project (WESP)–was composed of AFDC recipients and representatives from numerous advocacy organizations. In the winter of 1994, members of WESP began to dialogue with academics–including one author of this article–about the type of research they felt was needed in order to inform the welfare debate in a way that represented the interests and perspectives of women and children. In particular, WESP's goal was to develop a "real" welfare reform agenda that acknowledged the economic difficulties encountered by single parents at home and in the labor market, and that gave voice to the concerns, aspirations, and trials of women currently on welfare.

From July 1994 to July 1995 three major research endeavors were carried out by WESP in order to gather data about why families go on welfare in Maine, and why, when they go off, they so often return. These projects were:

1. a mail survey of AFDC recipients (the AFDC Parent Survey), to find out about their work experience, their desire to work, and their history of AFDC receipt;
2. an analysis of the labor market to determine the characteristics of jobs available to women in Maine; and
3. focus group research with employers and former, current and potential AFDC recipients.

Findings from these research projects were disseminated widely to the public and to legislators.

The AFDC Parent Survey was constructed by members of WESP. It was a long survey—ten pages—and in its original form it was composed only of multiple choice and short answer questions (about 100 questions), focusing on employment history, perceived barriers to employment, and AFDC receipt history.

In order to access a random sample of AFDC families in the State of Maine, WESP approached the Department of Human Services (DHS) for assistance in sample selection. After reviewing the survey, DHS agreed to collaborate on selecting a sample and mailing the survey given the addition of two open-ended questions:

1. What are the most important things you are doing or could do to get off AFDC? and
2. What help do you need to do these things?

While the tone and focus of these questions would not have been the choice of WESP members, or these authors, as the best way to learn about the concerns and lives of women receiving AFDC, they did, nevertheless, allow respondents to tell their stories. In other words, the collaboration with DHS had the unexpected and ironic outcome of generating a rich source of narrative data which captured respondents' emotions, concerns, policy ideas, and life experiences in a way that the original survey of only close-ended questions could not. (WESP members added a third open-ended question: "Is there anything else you want to tell us?", which opened the door to even more narrative responses than the first two questions alone may have elicited.) This article presents a thematic analysis of that narrative data.

QUALITATIVE RESEARCH, FEMINIST RESEARCH, AND ONE AUTHOR'S EXPERIENCE WITH THE DATA

Qualitative Research

Qualitative research can be defined as research that produces descriptive data based upon written or spoken words or observable behavior

(Sherman & Reid, 1994). Qualitative research has often been seen as inferior to quantitative methods (Riessman, 1994; Reid, 1994; Toseland, 1994). Contributions from research based on qualitative methodologies have frequently been defined as trivial, fuzzy headed, or unscientific (Hartman, 1994). Yet qualitative studies can allow for a different sort of truth to be told. How truth is defined and how methods for truth seeking are chosen is highly political (Hartman, 1994). For too long truth has been defined by people who are distant from the experience. People who are debating over welfare reform know very little about what it is like to live on welfare or what it is like to try to leave the system. Hartman (1994), a social worker and researcher, believes progressive researchers have an obligation to facilitate the telling of life stories of oppressed and silenced people:

> We must listen to our clients and bring forth their wisdom, their lived experience, their visions of the world. As many of our clients have been powerless and oppressed their knowledge has been subjugated, their insights have been excluded from the discourse by those empowered to define the "truth": experts, professionals, editorial boards. (p. 462)

Feminist Research and One Author's Experience with the Data

The survey sought to gain the perspective of recipients about barriers to independence from AFDC. WESP was determined that the voices of AFDC recipients be heard in the debate over the fate of their lives. Social policy formulation rarely takes into account the perspectives of women (Davis, 1994). "Despite scholarship showing that women's exclusion from the development of social policy resulted in a social service system that is clearly inequitable and frequently harmful, policy researchers have not addressed the underrepresentation of women in this arena" (Spakes & Nichols-Casebolt, 1994, p. 363). The research carried out by WESP was guided by feminist principles and sought to include a feminist perspective in social policy development in the State of Maine.

Feminist methodology seeks to allow the stories of otherwise silenced people to be heard. It is grounded in the politics of oppression and trans-formation (Davis & Srinivasan, 1994).

> Those in power have sought to define reality for the community as a whole. They have often succeeded. At the core of feminist research, therefore, is the commitment to give voice to previously marginalized and silenced people. (Davis & Srinivasan, p. 348)

Three factors influenced the decision to analyze, synthesize and publish these narratives: the apparent need that the respondents had to reach out of their isolation to other women and tell their stories; the desire of respondents to participate in a debate of which they felt shut out and about which they had strong opinions; and most significantly, the power of the respondents' individual and collective voices. One author had the task of initially preparing the quantitative data on the surveys for data entry and while reading through the surveys she was struck by both the quantity and quality of the narrative data recipients had included.

The power of the data particularly resonated with this author as she identified with the respondents, having been a low-income single mother and welfare recipient for a period of time, thus sharing experiences in common with many AFDC recipients who had participated in the study. In addition to experience, the author shared a powerful dimension of single mother poverty expressed in the narratives: the alienation created by the prejudice society has toward the poor, and the projection of the culture onto her and others like her–poor mothers raising children–of negative stereotypes made up largely of lies and misinformation. The following three quotes from the surveys address this alienation and consequent feelings of confusion, doubt, anger and shame often expressed in the narratives:[1]

> Becoming involved with public assistance has been one of the most demeaning, tedious, upsetting and educational things I've had to do. I battle constantly with all the societal pros and cons I've internalized throughout my life. Am I just using excuses to keep from working? Will I ever really be successful enough to support myself and my daughter and is that possible these days, without a master's or husband? Am I as pathetic as I feel when those almighty DHS workers look at me?

> Being on the state is very degrading. I am the best mother I know, but I am looked down on because of my financial situation. I certainly didn't know when I had my children that I would be in this position. I am not lazy or dumb, I'm just poor.

> Just because I'm on the state doesn't mean I'm not human. Would you (the state) live the way we do in poor housing, unhealthy homes and barely getting by? Just let me see you do this for awhile. It's not easy.

This author was personally aware that for a mother struggling to raise a family well below the poverty line, it can feel like life is being lived behind a one-way mirror, parallel to but never touching everyone whose lives are connected to the system through sustaining employment, family resources, health insurance, etc. You can see them, but they cannot see you, and no matter what you do, you do not become visible to them. Respondents wrote about their sense of invisibility and powerlessness and their narratives were a plea to be seen and heard as real individual people and not stereotypes as illustrated by these three quotes:

> I have written a letter to President Clinton and told about my life from A to Z and received a nice reply but that was it. Also wrote a letter to Rep. Snowe's office and a reply came back with no solutions. I feel that people in government do not have a real understanding of people's needs, especially women and children.

> We are a part of the human race that didn't get that break in life, where you landed a great job that you can earn a lot, get great benefits, and your job is for life. I feel right now I'll never have anything and without welfare would be hungry too. Can't spell very good, low self-image and panic attacks, all this at twenty-five, and no need of it. Help me help myself and my children please.

> The prejudice needs to stop. One store I went into had an article titled, "Why Make Welfare Easier?" taped to the cash register. How can I shop there knowing they look down on me? People say whatever they want to me. I've had people try to tell me how to raise my daughter. I am a certified nursery school teacher but that doesn't seem to matter to them. I've had people tell me I'm a bad mother because I put my daughter in time out but won't spank her. People walk up to me in the grocery store and tell me what they believe I'm doing wrong. Attitudes need to change.

Feminist methodology, along with other postempirical theories, postulates that the investigator is invariably located both socially and historically and that this context influences the knowledge being produced. Proponents argue that there is no such thing as a wholly objective or disinterested perspective and reject the assumption that a strict separation between researcher and subject produces a more valid, objective account (Neilsen, 1990). This methodology considers the woman, not the researcher, to be the expert on her own experience, and makes the assumption that we have a great deal to learn from women's stories, which may challenge prevailing notions (Neilsen, 1990).

Recipients themselves have been largely locked out of the debate over welfare reform. Given the current political climate, it is imperative that the material in narratives such as these be put forward so that respondents' experiences and points of view can be heard. A postempirical theory relevant to feminist methodology, standpoint epistemology, postulates that the less powerful members of society have the potential for a more complete view of social reality because of their disadvantaged position. The oppressed know their oppressors as a matter of survival; however, the reverse is not true. Furthermore, the dominant and subordinate groups will tend to have inverted views, which has often been the case in the welfare debate (Hartsock, 1983). An example of this is that in the narrative data women repeatedly stated that they wanted to work, were in a job search or were doing involuntary part-time work while searching for full-time work, or had had to quit work because wages were too low and they did not have access to health insurance. However, the debate by lawmakers is dominated by the belief that a central problem is that welfare recipients do not want to work and must be forced into the job market. Publishing the words of these women is one response to the alienation and invisibility they reflected in their writings; they are the experts in the welfare debate from whom policy makers, and all of us, have a lot to learn.[2]

METHOD

The questionnaire was mailed to 3,000 AFDC families in the State of Maine in September of 1994; this was about 14 percent of the 21,066 AFDC families in the state at that time. Nine hundred and twenty nine surveys were returned, giving an overall response rate of 31 percent. Data from the short answer questions were coded and entered into a data management program. The data set was imported into *Systat for Windows* for further quantitative data analysis.

While 31 percent is a fairly low return rate, it is not surprising given that the survey questionnaire was extremely long–11 pages, with over 100 multiple choice questions in addition to the three open-ended questions–and that no follow-up phone calls or correspondence were conducted to increase the response rate. While a cover letter from the Women's Economic Security Project (WESP) was included with the questionnaire, it is possible that recipients of the survey overlooked this letter and assumed the research originated from the Department of Human Services (DHS)–an agency from which many had experienced harassment; such an assumption may have discouraged some recipients from filling out what appeared to be yet another lengthy form. Those respondents who returned the surveys did so very quickly and appeared to have a considerable amount to say. It is possible that this sample of 929 AFDC recipients differs from the entire population of recipients in Maine in their desire to have their voices heard. Nearly all of the respondents took the time to answer the open-ended questions. Many respondents attached multiple pages in order to write all they had to say.

An independent thematic analysis was done by each author using coding procedures as described by Strauss and Corbin (1990). On several occasions the authors compared and discussed emerging themes. The independent analyses corroborated one another; in fact there was surprising consistency in how each author interpreted the data and created categories, lending trustworthiness to the final analysis. By contrasting and comparing each author's independent analysis, thematic categories were easily negotiated and labeled. These resulting themes and supporting data are presented below.

RESULTS

Sample

Of the 929 respondents, 891 (95.9%) were women. Only 5.4% (n = 50) were under 20 years of age. Most respondents (n = 639, 68.8%) were between the ages of 20 and 34. The average number of children per family was 1.85. Only 57 families had more than three children (6.1%). One hundred and twenty four respondents (13.3%) were married, 332 (35.7%) were unmarried, 12 (1.3%) were widowed, and the rest were separated or divorced (n = 461, 49.7%). Two hundred and five respondents (22.1%) had less than a high school diploma, 447 (48.3%) had obtained a high school diploma or General Equivalency Degree (GED), 225 (24.3%) had some college or technical school, and the remainder, 42 (5.2%), had at least a college degree (Women's Development Institute, 1995).

At the time of the survey, 199 respondents (21.5%) were employed outside the home; nearly three quarters of the respondents (n = 672, 73.2%) had worked in the preceding five years. The average hourly wage of the respondents in the sample who had worked in the preceding 12 months was $5.37. Most respondents (81.6%) were concentrated in three low wage occupations: sales, services, and administrative support. Only 15.6% of the jobs held by respondents provided health insurance they could afford (Women's Development Institute, 1995).

Themes

Concepts which emerged in the data were grouped under six major thematic categories. Each category was given a primary and secondary title descriptive of the concepts grouped within. The thematic categories developed were: (1) Struggling against odds/(women bear the burden); (2) Children are the priority/(not any child care will do); (3) Catch-22/ (not any job will do); (4) Give us a chance/(it is a long way from here to there); (5) Division of the oppressed/(blaming the victim); and (6) Thank you for listening/(isolation). Each thematic category will be described below through the voices of the respondents.

Struggling Against Odds/(Women Bear the Burden)

The data gave clear testimony of how difficult life was for many of these women. Some had dealt with abusive partners and, while glad to be free from the abuse, struggled to survive as single parents. Others were disabled–often from employment injuries–and unsure whether they'd be able to survive without AFDC. All of the respondents struggled to meet basic expenses with the small amount they received through AFDC and whatever employment income or child support they might also periodically receive. Many women were angry at the fathers of their children who provided little to no support and at the system which, in their eyes, was not working hard enough to make the men pay.

While no longer living with daily battering in their current lives, two women who were victims of abuse by the fathers of their children continued to struggle to bring up their children as single mothers:

> I got married at age 19–became a housewife and mom for 10 years and live to talk about it. I've had an abusive 10 years and finally got out. Now for the last four years, I'm still struggling to raise my children alone. I don't feel stable enough to try to afford raising the children with a minimum pay job, with probably no car to do it with or funds to improve it.

> I never would have gotten on AFDC again except I got laid off and ended up in the hospital twice this summer and couldn't work for two months 18 months ago. My son's dad tried to kill me four times. We spent last summer in court. He did some time in jail and now he says I'll never see child support. Thus far we are still in court for mediation and child support . . . I just don't understand the system. I can be beat on, shot at, and have my son kidnapped and taken away to Canada and all he gets is 5 days in jail and enough money from his boss to keep fighting me in court. I'm tired of fighting them and now I owe so much to everyone and I have no money to pay hospital payments, lawyer bills or a bank payment that I co-signed two years ago. The man says he doesn't want to pay anymore so I have to.

As the previous story illustrates, many women go on AFDC due to health problems. These women are coping with failing health, bringing up children on their own, and trying to meet basic living expenses with very little money. Two examples of what life is like for disabled women on AFDC follow:

> I wish there was help out there for people that are really trying like myself. I tried very hard not to have to go back on AFDC. I have two children neither father pays child support and three months ago I was told I had bone marrow cancer and could die. I went to get help because I can not work 40 to 45 hours a week because of the illness and treatments and they told me I can only receive AFDC of $346 a month, $170 food stamps, and Medicaid. (Medicaid is a life saver.) I also work between 20 and 25 hours a week and bring home about $120 a week. How can I do it? I don't live on housing of any kind and it is about another year before I can get any housing help so I have to pay $575 a month in rent that leaves me about $250 a month to pay lights, phone, day care, gas to borrow someone's car and everything else. I cannot get that much city help. So where do I go from here?

> I am disabled, I cope, the future isn't so bright, but I dwell on now and how to make every minute special for my family and myself. My family needs the AFDC and food stamps just to survive in America. I am on heavy medication and will be on it for the rest of my life unless God changes it.

Many women spoke of how hard it was to balance working or school with the responsibilities of being a single parent. They indicated how difficult it was to find employment that was flexible enough to accommodate the needs of a single parent, or to finish training or education programs which didn't allow for the demands of single parenting. One woman became homeless the last time she worked at low-wage work; the only job in her area that paid enough would not allow her to be with her children:

> I've gone off AFDC to work. It didn't pay enough or no insurance and then became homeless with three children. I haven't worked since, hoping to be able to go to school, so that the next time I go off I'll stay off. My self-esteem would be better if I was off the program, but I have to feed my children also . . . I can't do mill work because I won't see my children during the school year. I did that for a year in

the past. I have two pre-teenage daughters that need me at home each night. Mill work is the only job that would pay enough to go off AFDC, and I really would like to go off AFDC and have a life of self-worth. Have a life.

Another woman worked two low-wage jobs despite unreliable transportation and few opportunities for advancement:

> I work two jobs. As a CNA-CRMA [certified nursing assistant] and as a PCA [personal care attendant]. My car breaks down continually. I want to go to school to get my LPN. That way I can earn more money doing what I love. I was told there was nothing out there to help me.

Even those women fortunate to get assistance for training or education had to deal with the daily demands of being a single parent, making it difficult to finish training programs in limited periods of time:

> I know how difficult it is to continue an education as a single parent. It would have been impossible to have completed the course requirement in two years. Single parents are under enough stress. Forcing them into a situation that offers education in two years would offer too much stress. Children would suffer under a program that is designed to help them. As long as a single parent in school is progressing toward a diploma or degree, they should receive aid. Part of my problem is that once matriculated I had to complete my education in 104 weeks. That wasn't enough time to study sufficiently.

Many women spoke of how they were left "holding the bag." They did not conceive these children alone, but they were in fact raising them alone with little to no support from their children's fathers. Three women, angry about their situation, wrote:

> My ex-husband has not been forced to abide by any of the things stated in my divorce decree. The only reason I get child support is because he is working (for now). But he will soon quit as he always does. He has been through several jobs in the last few years and once the state starts garnishing his wages he quits. Recently he kidnapped my children and accused me of welfare fraud (made a report to the state). I have gotten my children back and I'm not sure what the state will do about his bogus accusations . . . The fathers that walk out on these children must be made to pay. It seems like this man can do

anything to me and my children and get away with it. This scares me, I never know what is next.

I've been on the state for three years and have never received any money from the father. He has never done a thing for my child but I'm the one that gets laughed at and talked about behind my back. All he gets is pats on the back for being a father and having a child. I'm the one that deals with my child's pain, happiness, and his sadness. But I don't get a pat on the back. Things seem a little messed up.

Parents who don't pay child support should be put in jail or forced to work off the child support for the state reimbursement. These parents that walk away, paying no child support and having no responsibility, leave the entire emotional load on one parent who is forced into poverty and struggle.

Some women felt as though the state was not working actively enough to obtain the child support owed by their children's fathers. These women believed it was wrong that their children were suffering while the non-paying fathers were escaping without punishment. As two women pointed out:

I did not get pregnant by myself. My ex-husband is the father of all three of my youngest children. My ex-husband had a job working for a painting contractor in town and when the state sent a letter to attach his pay he quit his job. I don't feel that it's right to push the mothers out of the home and do nothing to absent parents. My ex is working for another painter and Support Enforcement is trying to catch up with him. *He owes the State of Maine over $35,000!* Why doesn't someone threaten him with jail time? We certainly could use the child support.

And no help from my ex-husband is another source of grief. The state says they're going after dead beat fathers but it's a lie to please us mothers for awhile and it doesn't please me. So I can't win for losing. I feel like I'm an outcast of society! And society makes me feel like dirt to ask for help.

Many women listed out their basic expenses for rent, food and heat to demonstrate that it was impossible to make ends meet with AFDC and food stamps. For example, some spoke of doing without meals so their children could eat, or not buying oil for heat and being cold in the winter in order to pay the rent. They wondered why anyone would think they liked living on AFDC when it was such a struggle to survive. One woman said that she would like

> for the people who make up the rules for AFDC to see how really hard it is to be a single parent trying to make ends meet and have a nice home for kids on what they say you should be able to live on.

Despite the shame and discomfort of being on AFDC, women really saw that they had no choice. One of the primary purposes in their lives—many would say *the* primary purpose—was to provide for their children, and they were receiving welfare for that very reason. That their children were the priority in their lives was reiterated time and again by the respondents.

Children Are Priority/(Not Any Child Care Will Do)

The nature of the question: "What are the most important things you are doing or could do to get off AFDC?" forced a certain type of answer. This question—added by the Department of Human Services—presumed that women should be trying to get off welfare; thus respondents had to defend their desire to stay at home with their children. One woman wrote very eloquently about the double standard in our society: poor women are supposed to work while wealthier women are given permission and encouragement to stay home with their children:

> I can not believe how many people are considering forcing women off AFDC after two years. We, as a society, are willing to encourage mothers to stay home with their children unless they are poor women. We even blame many of society's problems on women being in the work place instead of staying home except if they are poor women. We are willing to admit how many women are stressed to the limit trying to work and still do all the rest unless they are poor single women on AFDC. No thought is given to how much harder this will be for someone without a partner. I especially can't believe this could even be considered without major changes in the child care situation. There needs to be adequate quality affordable day care made available. There also needs to be jobs that a person can survive working at with wages that allow one to live above the poverty line. More flexible hours on jobs and sick leaves in case of a child becoming ill are also needed. Insurance also. I guess what I feel needs to be instilled in our society is a basic concern for the well-being of this country's women and children. I don't feel this exists now.

As the above quote indicated, the lack of adequate, affordable, available child care in many areas of the state is a severe problem for low-income women considering entering the work force. Along with the fear of losing the health insurance provided by Medicaid, locating suitable, affordable child care appeared to be one of the primary obstacles for women considering employment. They were not willing to leave their children with "just anyone" as illustrated by this quote:

> I need health insurance for my son. I would also need help with a baby-sitter. I cannot have just "anyone" care for my child because he needs one-on-one supervision. I cannot lose his Medicaid card because he requires a great deal of health care.

One woman, who was involved in a custody battle with the abusive father of her son, felt she was not ready to leave her children during the day. She asked for

> some reliable day care suggestions, and me to feel comfortable that what I'd be doing was right for my kids and would help me in the long run, not make things worse.

Some women felt like day care was clearly an inferior choice to staying at home, as illustrated by the following quote:

> People don't realize when you have young children how much it costs for day care, and that a lot of times it would be easier to wait to get a job after the kids are all in school. Also nowadays with all the sick people in the world, it is a scary thing to leave your child with some one and not know if they are going to hurt your child. You can't really trust anyone any more.

As mentioned by the above respondent, women were very cautious about leaving their children with strangers, especially if their children were already emotionally traumatized. As one respondent wrote:

> I would need to work around my son and have a sitter he would be feeling safe with. Right now he doesn't even feel safe in school due to his father showing up there. I would like to really be able to work at home so I can be there for my son. My child, besides his emotional problems, gets sick a lot during the school year. Children need their parent there for them especially a child that has been abused. My son is nine and he still messes his pants both ways when he feels fearful and stressed. He sees a family and individual counselor each week.

Due to the fear of abuse by strangers, several women spoke of postponing the time when their children would be out of their direct and constant care. The three following quotes exemplify this caution:

> I'm not ready [to stop getting AFDC]. My kids, excluding the youngest, have been sexually abused in the past. I can't trust anyone. So it's better to stay home with them yourself. I'm not going through it again.

> I would feel better if I went to work and left my children with a baby-sitter when they were at least able to walk and talk. That way if something bad is happening to them, they could at least tell me about it.

> As for right now, I am not going to work out of my home until the start of school next year. I do more for my child than a daycare or preschool can. I won't trust that kind of resource.

Other women thought that being home with their small children was more important than working. This philosophy was illustrated by the following quote:

> Right now I'm not doing anything because I'm pregnant and am going to want to stay home with my newborn once it arrives for at least one or two years. . . . an infant's first one or two years of life are very important, not only for the mother but for the child themself.

> It's very hard to be a single mom. In order to support myself and my daughter, I need more money than AFDC gives me. I need to work part-time now. Then do school at night, later with work during the day . . . when is there time for my daughter? She'll be tossed around all the time and she won't even know who I am, anymore. Work and school are important, but my daughter is more important, and she'll be missing out on having her mom around. My mom did that to me. It hurts!

As mentioned under the preceding theme, many AFDC recipients responding to the survey were disabled and unable to work; similarly a substantial number of respondents spoke of caring for disabled children. This can be full-time work in itself, and actually far cheaper for the government than funding specialized care. Some of these parents have become experts in the field of special needs children and would have a hard time finding affordable child care to replace their own services. As two mothers of special needs children explained:

Parents of disabled children have the demands of a full-time job just to keep home and family safe and healthy. Child care centers for disabled children are not an adequate choice as most people are not familiar with the problems associated in raising children with autism as we are learning facts about the condition of autism on a day to day basis. New strategies/technology for autistic children is in experimental stages right now and few are on the cutting edge of this affliction.

I would have to get reliable transportation and child care. I need someone willing to put my four year old daughter on a breathing machine three times a day.

Some respondents were very creative in envisioning work situations and child care arrangements that would work for them. Generally this involved flexible work schedules or working at home. One respondent laid out three scenarios which would allow her to deal with the problems of being an employed single parent:

I'm a very devoted mother and would prefer to be here for my kids at all times. It's hard for me to feel fully comfortable with baby sitters or daycares. However I feel I need and want to get a full time job that pays well. The ideal situation for me would be to work graveyard shift and hire someone to sleep at my home five nights a week. Then I'd be home before and after school and on sick days and holidays, and during the summer. Getting enough sleep could be a problem in the summer though. Another option would be if I could find some kind of work that I could do at home like some sort of assembly work. The third option would be the government opening up free day care centers for low income people that have highly qualified care givers and nurses on hand for sick child caregiving as well. This could perhaps save the government money provided there were enough jobs available for AFDC recipients.

Many of the women wondered at the logic of paying a child care provider to watch their children so they could work for a small income, much of which would go to the child care costs. At the same time they would be losing quality time with their children and be no better off—and sometimes worse off—financially. This was often labeled as "catch-22" by the respondents.

Catch-22/(Not Any Job Will Do)

Nearly three quarters of the respondents had been employed in the preceding five years. Most of these respondents spoke of how difficult it was to stay employed. The cost of day care, the loss of medical insurance, and the immediate cut in benefits all served to make working at low-wage jobs a more costly choice than staying on AFDC. Many felt anger that the system seemed to be working against them, and that they were trapped on welfare despite their efforts to get off. The following three respondents explained this trap:

> If you do not have a degree or even diploma at minimum wage there is no way she [a single mother] can afford child care, rent, electricity, heat, insurance on a car to get to work. All on $140 a week. It is much easier for them [single mothers] to stay home with the security. What I mean by that is you're sure you're gonna at least have food from food stamps, medical from Medicaid, and a monthly check that does not have to go mostly to a child care provider. Also, that your child is being cared for properly, because you are the one that's doing it.

> Specifically, I don't think it's fair for the rent to increase, food stamps to decrease, and the electric bill to be so incredibly high. Once I start work the medical insurance comes to a halt and this makes it just as hard. I'm doing this to give my boys a good, healthy life, but it seems no matter how hard I try, something gets cut. I'm not the kind of person who will make AFDC a living, this is why I went to college and received a degree.

> If the government wouldn't take all the benefits the minute you make $600 a month, it would give a lot of people more incentive to get off AFDC and stay off it.

Current welfare reform emphasizes putting welfare recipients to work at any job they can get. Advocates for low-income women, and low-income women themselves, argue against such reform given the evidence that one cannot raise a family on minimum wage work, and that there is a dearth of jobs offering livable wages for low-skilled, or even college-educated, individuals. Many respondents spoke to this issue, as illustrated by the following three quotes:

> The job market has been very poor and it has been difficult to find good paying job with even my college education. Very few jobs are

40 hours a week and a lot of part-time work has no benefits. Being a single parent with only one income coming in the household requires full-time work to have a decent life for your children. AFDC is also no help. When you do get a job they take everything away almost immediately when you start a job instead of helping you until you get on your feet.

I am tired of being on state aid but find that they make it hard for me to get off of it. They expect us to take a job for $5.00 [an hour] and work our butts off for $5.00 an hour plus have child care expenses then we have to come home and take care of our children and personally a lot of us women would rather stay home and take care of our children for the money we get from the state. It would be a different story if I could get a job for $8.00 an hour and still help from the state. But either way you people find a way to make us struggle and keep us down.

I tried to get off AFDC and I worked full time at $4.65 an hour and after my weekly bills of rent, child care, phone bill, transportation, etc. I couldn't even afford to get insurance to get my daughter and I off of Medicaid. I do not receive child support at all and my daughter is 20 months old. I feel as if he is just enjoying his life [the father of the baby].

These women who have had to budget so carefully to survive on the low benefits which they receive from AFDC, realize, when they do the math, that going to work is just not affordable. In other words, there is a cost to going to work that often out-weighs the total wages earned. One woman calculates that child care is just too expensive:

It's not very comforting to a welfare parent who is trying to do right by wanting to work, that they get penalized for any extra money they make. Specifically if that "extra" isn't enough to help, but enough to hurt. One daycare facility that I looked into wanted $90 to $100 per child 5 days a week, 51 weeks paid plus paid holidays. (Includes two weeks paid vacation for staff.) $1.00 a minute for each minute late to pick up. A $5.00 hour job 40 hours a week would barely cover daycare.

The fear of losing Medicaid is a primary disincentive to go to work for many women. Only 15 percent of the recipients who had worked in the past 12 months were in employment that offered health insurance benefits that they could afford (Women's Development Institute, 1995). One respondent speaks of quitting her job to get Medicaid coverage when she had a medical problem:

> I do have to say that when I was working full time at my most recent job of four and a half years I had a very hard time making ends meet raising two children on my own. I barely received any financial assistance, some food stamps and medical cards for the kids. When I found out I needed foot surgery I had no insurance at work and Medicaid said I made too much money to receive benefits to help me have my surgery. So I ended up having to leave my job to get a medical card so that I could have my operation. That is a backwards system!

Other women are afraid of the consequences for themselves and their children if they lose Medicaid benefits through entering the low-wage job market. This fear is voiced by the following two respondents:

> I've worked at manual labor jobs for low pay since I was 15. Shoe shops, factory and nursing homes as a CNA. Due to back trouble, I can no longer perform this kind of work. The only work I am qualified for now is entry-level. These jobs are only part-time and you aren't eligible for health insurance unless you are management and sometimes not even then. When my kids were small I was terrified they'd get sick or seriously injured and I couldn't afford medical treatment. Child care was so expensive and pay was low. I couldn't afford to work. It cost me more to work! Welfare is like a trap.

> This is not what I want for my life—to receive state or local aid. But I am trapped here. I know for a fact that I couldn't make it without Medicaid. I take Prozac, Amitriptyline, Zantac, Taganet, Propulsid, and birth control pills every day! It would be impossible to pay for them even if insurance covered 70 percent, and I would be very unhealthy—possibly dead—without them. I don't like my situation any more than the taxpayers do, but I am doing the best I can with what I have.

Many AFDC recipients who do work outside their homes carefully monitor their hours and wages so that they will not lose all their benefits. Two examples of this active surveillance follow:

> I was working 24 hours a week and getting support. I could get by with no help and when my ex stopped paying child support I did not

qualify for benefits. They made it so I had to get a lesser job to get the help I needed. When the state catches up to my ex and I get my child support I will go out and try to get a job in my field. These jobs are hard to come by and I was very angry that I could not get help and keep my job while they went after my ex.

I've tried–the more I work the more they cut me. So I try to just work enough so they won't cut me too bad. I think the system really sucks. They get you in a rut, and you can't do too much or you lose your benefits! I swear they want you on this program until your kids are 18.

As the preceding quote indicates, many respondents did wonder if there was a conspiracy by the state to keep them stuck on "the system." From their perspective demands were being made of them without the means to meet those demands. Some of this anger and suspicion comes through in the following three quotes:

Any help would be wonderful, but I'm to the point where I believe all the state wants to do is yell and complain and take things away. They're not really interested in helping. If they could pass the problem off on someone else they would, and then close their eyes and act like the problem doesn't exist.

Governor McKernan wants AFDC recipients either in school or employed, yet does not provide me with the means to do it! The amount of money I receive barely covers our expenses so I am unable to save. I cannot pay child care expenses to search for a job, let alone for the first month back to work–and yet–I have to find a way. I don't know how he can make such proclamations without providing a means to accomplish it.

Once you get a job and let the people at DHS know you have a job they cut all your benefits back to nothing and you never have a chance to get ahead. They expect you to be able to save money out of what they give you a month (which for one parent and child is $312). That itself isn't enough to last the month. I'm not asking DHS to give more money, I just need them to give me a chance to get a job and get on my feet. That's half the reason I haven't gotten a job because I can't afford one because of the way DHS runs things.

One respondent mentions a state worker–who seems to have understood the "catch-22" phenomenon–suggesting to her that she'd be better off if she didn't work as she paid most of her income to child care. She found this situation very discouraging:

> I myself have had state workers ask me "why do you work if you're only grossing $90 a week and paying out $64 for child care?" I did this summer. For self-respect and a feeling of worth. If I could make it without collecting AFDC and I had an incentive I would do it. People stay on AFDC because it's easier. The state does nothing to help AFDC people who are trying to get off. After a while you get in a rut and think why bother?

A final quote captures the anger at being blamed for the country's financial woes and the catch-22 reality of being stuck in a trap no matter how one tries to "get off the state":

> I'm tired of having politicians blame the state and country's financial mess on welfare recipients and unplanned pregnancy in young women. The fact is it does happen and will continue to happen. Women on state aid need a way out. Being on state aid is like being stuck in a circle with no end. I don't believe anyone enjoys it. Who enjoys not having enough money to pay their bills or worrying about putting food on the table when their stamps run out? I don't know anyone who gets enough aid to cover the bills or food costs. However I do know women who have tried to get off welfare and have been forced to go back on for these reasons: They couldn't afford to take their children to the doctor's when they got sick; couldn't afford daycare costs–which average $15 a day–almost half of their pay check went to day care. That leaves those of us who can earn only minimum wage $100 a week if we're lucky. That's $400 a month to pay bills, buy clothes, food etc. and that is an impossible task.

Despite the anger and discouragement, some respondents had ideas about how the system could work better and what they would need to become self-supporting. They asked that they be given a real chance to get off of AFDC.

Give Us a Chance/(It Is a Long Way From Here to There)

Respondents asked for concrete tools–such as education–to assist them in becoming economically self-sufficient and for more time to "get back on their feet." They wanted to be treated with respect and given a real chance to succeed.

Allow us to get on our feet. Many respondents who spoke of the "catch-22" situation of trying to leave AFDC through paid employment had policy suggestions about how to make the transition off welfare a more likely event. Generally, as the two following quotes illustrate, they suggested that benefits be cut more slowly once an individual had income from employment:

> The state always takes away from you when you're trying to get ahead. They could help by giving you the AFDC (the same) for lets say six months so you don't have to go back on the state.

> I have been on AFDC since my oldest child was born. I don't like it but there is nothing I can do at this time. If somehow the state would work with us and when someone gets a full-time job let them keep AFDC and food stamps until they have worked 3 or 4 months so they can have help until things get adjusted. I hope something positive comes out of welfare reform and I hope I am one to be helped because I hate the situation I am in.

One respondent even offered a six point plan:

1. not have benefits cut while in school even if you have a work study job.
2. first three months receive same benefits.
3. next three months no AFDC, food stamps cut in half and still Medicaid.
4. next six months food stamps cut in half but still get Medicaid.
5. Medicaid for three years after start of job.
6. This is so the first year gives a person time to adjust to the change of once a month stuff to once a week or every two weeks. Plus relieves pressure for the first year. Plus gives time for the person to stock up on things, pay bill or catch up on bills.

The phrase "allow us to get on our feet" was used repeatedly. Respondents asked for patience and more support as they moved into the labor market. Two examples of this request follow:

> The state shouldn't take everything away from you, they should continue to help you until at least you stand without falling.

> I would like to see AFDC give us more support until we get back on our feet. (In other words let us stay on AFDC for about 4 to 5 months more when we go to work so we can get back on our feet.)

Numerous respondents considered working at home to be a good way to solve the child care problem. Some women had already begun small businesses, others had ideas of what they would like to do, though lack of funding was often a stumbling block. This entrepreneurial spirit is illustrated by the following two quotes:

> Two years ago I took an opportunity to start a new non-profit. It is a home for pregnant and parenting teens (12-19). I have made a lot of sacrifices including my salary, but it will pay off in salary, position, and experience. I need time and would like more business education. [I also need] funding for our program so maybe I can get paid and off AFDC.

> I am trying to begin a home and party business and I sew at home so that I don't have to pay child care. I would like to operate a craft business. I need a loan to start a craft business that would be low interest rate with a clause stating that if the business failed in the first year it would be considered a gift and I wouldn't owe the money back.

We need education. The importance of education and training was reiterated time and time again by survey respondents. Some of the respondents needed considerable support—both concrete and emotional—to gain the skills necessary for jobs that paid adequate wages. The road to economic self-sufficiency for these women would take an investment of time and resources. The following quotes exemplify some of the help women said they needed in order to move off of AFDC:

> I would like to get a job that would give me financial security. In order to get off AFDC I would need more schooling and a chance to prove myself. [I would need] money for training and psychological support to gain back more self esteem.

> [I need to] get a better education. Find a good job with good pay and good benefits, such as health and dental insurance. [I need] financial help. Get pointed in the right direction on where and how to start . . . I wish there was a way I could get an education, a good job and not depend on the state. But it's real scary. However I do plan on going back to school and try to become something.

> [I] would like some education program to learn something that would last a lifetime. [I need] all that is available: transportation, child care, money, food, medical.

I believe that something should be done to help train people on welfare so we can get off it. If I went out and got a job with what skills I have I wouldn't make enough to pay my child care or transportation. To say the least I am stuck in the welfare system and I don't see a way out. I hope you do something to help me and every person who has to live like me.

After I get my [high school] diploma I would like to go to college, but I would need assistance with transportation, child care, and the cost of going to college.

Many respondents spoke of being on the waiting list for the ASPIRE program (Maine's JOBS program). While politicians speak often about making recipients sign up for education and job programs, in actuality there are far more recipients anxious for this help than there are resources to help them. Respondents often seemed to be in a constant state of waiting, as exemplified by the following quote:

I'm trying to get help from the ASPIRE program so I can attend a six month (or less) program at Eastern Maine Technical College, for child care certification. (Child Development courses, etc.) Am anxious for this to work out. Was (am) on waiting list for education assistance from TDC (Training Development Corporation). No luck—*long* waiting lists.

The respondents who had been lucky enough to receive enriched services and training spoke of what a significant difference it made in their ability to move toward self-sufficiency. Two examples of this appreciation follow:

I just recently got access to transportation. Without transportation I had no hope to have a better life for myself and my children. Also I live in transitional housing, nice apartments that poor people can afford. Also the housing regulation is that you see a case management worker weekly. She has given me a lot of information on programs that have helped me and my children have a chance at a better life. I believe that without these types of housing and training programs, the poor would not have a chance at a better life.

I am going to EMTC [technical college] for CDA [child development assistant] training. When I finish training I will have my CDA. Then I can open my own daycare or work as a teacher for Head Start. ASPIRE is giving me a lot of help.

One respondent mentioned her fear that her benefits would be cut before she finished her program:

> I'm now going to CMTC [technical college] in the electronics program. I do believe it is the best program to be in with the way things are going with technology. Don't cut my AFDC and I can finish school.

Some respondents wanted a chance to prove themselves. They felt that if they were given the opportunity they could do good work, but those opportunities seemed hard to come by. The following quotes are from three respondents who asked that someone take a chance on them:

> My schooling is being paid for by Voc. Rehab. and Pell grants and loans. I would love for someone to take a chance on me and hire me or give me training. I'm a very personable, likable, and smart person. Most places I've applied to want more experience, at least two years of paid experience. How can I get the experience if nobody will hire me?

> [I wish] some of these jobs around here would give people a chance at trying to do the work. Most of them want experienced people. But there are some people out there that don't have experience and they won't give them the chance to try.

> I've been trying to get into TDC, a school for people who are on AFDC etc. The most important things to get off AFDC would be to go to school for hair design and get a job. First I need to be accepted by the school and at least get the chance to prove I can do this and get myself back on track with the real world!

Some respondents wrote of their desire for a gentler approach from their caseworkers. They asked for guidance, and emotional support, and to be treated with respect. These requests are exemplified in the following four quotes:

> I don't feel that being on welfare is enjoyable for most people, but it is often viewed as such. What is needed is a helping hand not a hand out, for recipients to be shown how to help themselves and not be penalized for doing so, and for each person to be treated respectfully.

> At this point it all seems so hopeless, I go from day to day and try not to think about it. Deep inside I feel maybe there's a way out but I just

can't see it. [I need] direction not threats! Feeling of support not fear of losing everything. Guidance. Then possibly training and school.

Me, personally, I need someone to help every step. Someone to talk to if I have questions or need help. Plus information to help get started on whatever we choose to do.

They should help people on AFDC with training for a job or prepare for further education. Some people on AFDC don't choose to be on it but have no other choice. The state or a social worker should interact with the people more. Maybe set up appointments so people can go in and talk with someone. See what their options are.

One respondent who asked for emotional support as well as concrete assistance with child care, education and transportation stated that it is lack of confidence which traps many recipients:

I feel that AFDC recipients are ashamed of themselves and feel *very* helpless and *un-normal*. They lack confidence and motivation because of the position they are in and from society.

This overall theme of "give us a chance" and specifically these final quotes illustrate the obstacles AFDC recipients face in their lives. It is interesting that as they ask for patience and understanding from society, policy makers, and caseworkers, that they might also need to ask for empathy from their fellow AFDC recipients. The next theme captures how the victim blaming discourse around welfare reform has been absorbed by some of the recipients themselves.

Division of the Oppressed/(Blaming the Victim)

Compared to the previous themes, there were far fewer respondents whose narratives fell into this "division of the oppressed" category. Fewer than five percent of the respondents spoke disparagingly about other welfare recipients. But their remarks were striking and warrant attention. People who labeled other recipients as lazy, or liars, or in need of stricter rules, seemed to set themselves apart: they, themselves, were among the decent, hard working, honest people, while these other people they knew were abusing the system. Often a respondent would list the reasons *she* was not working on one page–e.g., lack of child care, transportation, health care, good paying jobs–and on the next page, sermonize about the women who just stay home and have babies. As a result of the "scapegoating" in the media, among politicians and the public, and perhaps due to personal experience with someone abusing the system, some recipients expressed concern that sanctions might be put in place that would harm all families on welfare. Other AFDC recipients appear to be an easy target for built up frustrations. Perhaps, as several respondents said, there is a hope that if the "bad ones" are "weeded out," there will be more of the pie left over for the "decent people." Examples of this blaming attitude appear in the following three quotes:

> I feel the entire welfare program should be revamped. I have seen (and closely known) people who abuse and defraud the welfare system so blatantly that I'm surprised they were never caught! I feel we have to weed out the people who see this as a lifestyle and adjust the benefits and training compensation/availability for those who truly want better and see welfare as just a stepping stone.

> I feel that there should be more investigators to check on welfare recipients for abuse of the system. I feel that when the system is abused the children pay the price and welfare recipients who are trying to raise their children properly or to the best of their ability also pay. They pay by being stereotyped as a welfare case. Or since there is so much abuse they need to cut back or not offer programs that may help people with good intentions.

> Seventy-five percent of people I personally know *deliberately* fraud the welfare system. They put down that more people live in their homes than do to get more money, food stamps, Medicaid, general assistance. They get fuel assistance and either cash the checks and spend the money on drugs and alcohol, or sell off their wood [used for heat in Maine] and want people to feel sorry for them. A lot of times they trade food stamps off for money to get alcohol and cigarettes. They say they're paying mortgages when they're not. The ones that are honest like myself are the ones who are denied benefits.

A few women come out strongly for time limits, "family caps," and stricter rules. They seem to have accepted the stereotypes of "welfare moms" while holding themselves out as exceptions. Three examples of this perspective follow:

> There are too many people living off the state and they shouldn't be. Especially the ones that have lived on it generation after generation. There is no need of it. I wasn't brought up on it and I'm not too

proud to be on it now. I think the state should let people be on it for a strict period of time and that's it. If people think that they can get it forever then they're not going to do anything with their lives.

I think you need to set up a program that people who go onto the state can only collect for two years. I know people who have been on the state for five to nine years. They stay on it because it's easier for them. They take advantage of this program and I believe that's why Maine has too many people on it. Make rules and stick to them. This state will never be any different unless someone puts their foot down on these people.

I feel the state shouldn't be paying for young girls having two or three kids before they are 18 years old. One, yes. This is why young girls have children so young because of the money. Yes I made a mistake [and had a child as a teenager].

Whether blaming other AFDC recipients for the problems with welfare, explaining their own struggles to survive, defending their choice to stay home with their children, recounting their futile efforts to survive on minimum wage work, or asking for more concrete and emotional assistance to overcome the multiple barriers to economic self-sufficiency, these survey respondents appeared grateful to have a platform from which to voice their views and tell their stories. They were glad someone had finally bothered to ask them what they thought.

Thank You for Listening/(Isolation)

Part of being oppressed is being silenced. Many respondents spoke of being denigrated by society and by the welfare system. The substantial response rate to the survey, and the fact that nearly all the respondents answered the narrative questions indicate this population's desire to be heard.

One respondent wrote eloquently about how her spirit had almost been broken by the treatment she had received from society. As a poor woman she had been cast off and isolated:

I'm doing nothing and have lost my desire–the desire that motivated me in the past–to go to school. It seems each time I've gotten to school (without the help of ASPIRE, etc.) my car has broken down beyond repair. I get another car and it craps out too. I feel as though my hands are tied. I've applied at Reny's [a discount department store] and wait with resignation to become a bag lady in old age–a bag lady with presence. . . . I feel sadder than sad that I can't see a way out and sometimes I feel so angry but neither sad or angry are productive–so with my time I read a lot, pray and hope a lot. Not for a knight in shining armor but for a better way–for a change in attitudes about people on welfare, for a system that doesn't need the poor to survive, and that no longer denigrates its host.

Respondents frequently referred to the humiliating treatment they received at DHS. They wanted to be heard and treated as human beings. These pleas are exemplified in the following two quotes:

[I want] not to be treated as a lesser of a person who is trying to abuse a system! The help I need is the help to be heard! AFDC workers treat recipients as imbeciles! We are people–yes some abuse–some like myself use the system for that intended!

I am going to school to get my social work degree, because of several reasons. One reason after dealing with DHS for several different reasons and different departments I feel that DHS does not care about their clients, have enough workers, and they are very degrading and humiliating to the clients they are serving. I am not out to stay on AFDC for the rest of my life. I want to make something of myself, as how I was put into this situation was really out of my control. I have the ability to understand what I need to do, but a lot of other clients do not have the abilities or the intelligence to help themselves. DHS needs people to help this type of client, to help these people. Just not every six months for recertification.

Time and again respondents thanked the researchers for providing a vehicle for them to air their views and experiences. The final comments on five surveys indicate this gratitude:

Thank you for creating this survey, it's nice to know someone thinks about our ideas on this subject. There are a lot of us who would like to get on with our lives as self-sufficient citizens.

I would like to say that I'm glad some kind of survey is being taken and I'm sure all AFDC mothers will have something to say.

This questionnaire is a very good way to find real solutions to the welfare problems. Welfare recipients are people too.

Thank you for the opportunity to blow off some steam! . . . Good luck with your project.

I am glad to answer this survey. I have many times wanted to express my reasons for *still* using AFDC. Thank you.

One respondent voiced strong skepticism that anything good could come of the survey:

What do you think you can do for us? I'm 47 and have fought this battle for years. I'm tired and have only contempt for the bureaucratic system. I don't want anything handed to me. Every time I've tried to pull myself up someone cuts the rope. Its a big joke but it certainly keeps all of you in a job! If you want to know how to help, come down and live at this level for a while.

Other respondents appeared more hopeful that their opinions and experiences would make a difference and that policy makers would take them seriously. These final three quotes reflect that view:

Thank you for letting me vent. I hope it does some good. I'm not the only one who feels this way.

I hope your efforts are heard.

I just hope that these pleas for help from the surveys you are receiving will be taken seriously. I also hope that it becomes even more apparent that not every AFDC recipient is taking advantage of the system. But merely victim of the system. For whatever reason.

DISCUSSION

The stories of these AFDC recipients paint a stark picture of the destitution and humiliation that can accompany life on welfare. The narratives document the resiliency and resourcefulness of the respondents to meet the needs of their children despite incredible obstacles. What becomes clear in the narratives is that, contrary to arguments that drive the welfare debate, mothers are often making the wisest choices from among those available to them in order to do what is best for their families. The respondents took parenting seriously, and they wanted to give the very best they could to their children. Moving into low-wage work was generally not the best option for meeting the needs of their families: they would lose quality time with their children; they would probably lose health insurance; and they might have less money to pay the bills.

Most respondents saw education and training as the route to the sort of employment that would provide sufficiently high wages and benefits so that they could raise their families without state aid. Rarely would a respondent mention that she wanted a "job," it was always that she wanted a "good paying job." While policy makers may not make this distinction, low-income parents do. Access to education and training has been limited in the State of Maine; respondents voiced frustration at being told to go to school or work only to find the resources weren't there to assist them when they tried. This frustration led to anger. Survey respondents were at times angry at the system that seemed to trap them, at times, at caseworkers who ignored them and humiliated them, and at times, at other AFDC recipients who they saw as undeserving of help due to certain bad behaviors.

Cook and Fonow (1990) list consciousness-raising as one of the primary principles of feminist research. While the survey instrument may have allowed some women to find relief in being able to finally tell their stories to someone who asked to hear them, it did not allow for dialogue. The isolation of poverty, compounded by the rurality of the State of Maine, has not allowed for a strong, state-wide welfare rights movement to form. Honkala (1995) of the National Welfare Rights Union emphasizes the importance of consciousness-raising in building a movement of poor people. The data from this survey indicate the power that stereotypes can have to divide some oppressed people—albeit a small number in this case—against one another as they fight for scarce resources.

CONCLUSION

Findings from the AFDC Parent Survey—primarily the quantitative data, though some quotes from the narrative data were also disseminated—were important in the state welfare debate during the 1995 legislative session. The survey results, along with the labor market analysis (Seguino, 1995) and the focus group research (Deatrick, 1995), provided the basis for a progressive welfare reform bill, An Act to Promote Work, Family and Dignity (L.D. 1389), introduced by State Representative Sharon Treat (An Act, 1995). There were numerous components to this bill, many of which mirrored the suggestions offered by the respondents of the AFDC Parent Survey. For example, among other things, L.D. 1389 allowed working parents to retain a declining level of cash assistance until they worked their way out of poverty; increased access to child care and transportation; provided more resources for education and training; increased the minimum wage; expanded access to health care for working parents under 150 percent of the poverty level; promoted "family friendly" work places by recognizing employers whose employment practices were responsive to the needs of families and children; and created a commission to examine how to balance the responsibility of the public and private sector in helping to raise working families out of poverty (An Act, 1995).

Activists from the advocacy, practitioner and AFDC recipient communities were mobilized on several occasions to testify and lobby their legislators in support of this bill and against many punitive initiatives introduced by the Independent governor's administration and Republican legislators. In all, there were eleven welfare reform bills introduced; these were primarily punitive in nature. At a full afternoon hearing of welfare reform bills before the Human Resources Committee, nearly all the testimony was in support of Representative Treat's bill. People supporting this positive welfare reform came from all over the state. Current and past AFDC recipients were present in large numbers and provided the most compelling testimony–eliciting questions and comments from legislators. Representatives from other communities in the state-wide coalition–including religious, labor, practitioner, and advocate–also spoke eloquently about how this bill would give welfare families a real chance to move out of poverty.

While L.D. 1389 did not pass, the state-wide coalition of advocates considered its work to be successful. Many harsher bills were defeated. For example: "drop dead" time limits–i.e., after a certain period of time no further assistance would be allowed under any circumstances–were not imposed though AFDC recipients will be required to work after two years of receiving benefits; a "family cap" was narrowly defeated; and a special housing needs allowance was retained. One aspect of L.D. 1389 which was incorporated into the final welfare reform legislation was the establishment of a commission to study poverty among working parents. The research projects already carried out by the Women's Economic Security Project–including the AFDC Parent Survey–provide a solid base from which the commission can work in the future. At the time of this writing, the full implications of implementing new federal welfare reform initiatives at the state level–e.g., block grants and five year time limits–are not known. We can only hope that the voices of AFDC recipients will continue to be heard in the ongoing debate over the fate of their lives and those of their children.

NOTES

1. The authors made minor corrections in grammar and spelling in all quotes when verbatim narrative was confusing; generally, however, the quotes are as the respondents wrote them.

2. Most survey respondents (95.9%) were women. The author's thematic analysis of narrative data included responses from female respondents only in order to give greater voice to women's perspective.

REFERENCES

Abramovitz, M. (1994). Challenging the myths of welfare reform from a woman's perspective. *Social Justice, 21* (1), 17-21.

Albelda, R. & Tilly, C. (1994). *Glass ceilings and bottomless pits: Women, income, and poverty in Massachusetts.* Boston: Women's Statewide Legislative Network.

Amott, T. (1994). Reforming welfare or reforming the labor market: Lessons from the Massachusetts employment training experience. *Social Justice, 21* (1), 33-37.

An Act to Promote Work Family and Dignity, L.D. 1389, 117th Maine Legislature, 1st Sess. (1995).

Center on Social Welfare Policy and Law. (1994). *Living at the bottom: An analysis of 1994 AFDC benefit levels.* Washington D.C.: Author.

Cloward, R. (1994). The workfare hoax. *Social Justice, 21* (1), 38-39.

Cook, J.A. & Fonow, M.M. (1990). Knowledge and women's interests: Issues of epistemology and methodology in feminist sociological research. In J.M. Nielsen, *Feminist research methods* (pp. 69-93). Boulder, CO: Westview Press.

Davis, L.V. (1994). Why we still need a women's agenda for social work. In L.V. Davis (Ed.), *Building on women's strengths: A social work agenda for the twenty-first century* (pp. 1-25). New York: The Haworth Press, Inc.

Davis, L.V. & Srinivasan, M. (1994). Feminist research within a battered women's shelter. In E. Sherman & W. Reid (Eds.), *Qualitative research in social work* (pp. 347-357). New York: Columbia University Press.

Deatrick, D.A. (1995). *The economic status of women in Maine: Focus group research.* Portland, ME: Edmund S. Muskie Institute.

Hagen, J.L. & Lurie, I. (1995). Implementing JOBS: From the Rose Garden to reality. *Social Work, 40* (4), 523-532.

Hagen, J.L. (1994). Public welfare and social work: New opportunities. In L.V. Davis (Ed.), *Building on women's strengths: A social work agenda for the twenty-first century* (pp. 57-79). New York: The Haworth Press, Inc.

Hartman, A. (1994). Setting the theme: Many ways of knowing. In E. Sherman & W. Reid (Eds.), *Qualitative research in social work* (pp. 459-463). New York: Columbia University Press.

Hartsock, N. (1983). The feminist standpoint: Developing the ground for a specifically feminist historical materialism. In S. Harding & M. Hintikka (Eds.), *Discovering reality* (pp. 283-310). Dordrecht, Holland: D. Reidel.

Honkala, C. (1995, June). Welfare reform: *Reaching the public and supporting each other in the fight.* Workshop at the national conference of the Bertha Capen Reynolds Society, Philadelphia, PA.

Jones, R.M. (1995). The price of welfare dependency: Children pay. *Social Work, 40* (4), 496-505.

Mageean, D. (1995). Welfare reform: What can work in Maine? In Maine Center for Economic Policy (Ed.), *Maine choices: 1995* (pp. 7-22). Augusta, ME: Editor.

Nielsen, J.M. (1990). Introduction. In J.M. Nielsen, *Feminist research methods* (pp. 1-37). Boulder, CO: Westview Press.

Parrott, S. (1995). *Cash assistance and related provisions in the Personal Responsibility Act (H.R. 4).* Washington DC: Center on Budget and Policy Priorities.

Rank, M.R. (1994). *Living on the edge: The realities of welfare in America.* New York: Columbia University Press.

Reid, W.J. (1994). Reframing the epistemological debate. In E. Sherman & W. Reid (Eds.) *Qualitative research in social work* (pp. 464-481). New York: Columbia University Press.

Riessman, C.K. (1994). Preface. In C.K. Riessman, *Qualitative studies in social work research* (pp. vii-xx). Thousand Oaks, CA: Sage Publications.

Seguino, S. (1995). *Living on the edge: Women working and providing for families in the Maine economy, 1979-1993.* Orono, ME: Margaret Chase Smith Center for Public Policy.

Sherman, E. & Reid, W.J. (1994). Introduction: Coming of age in social work–the emergence of qualitative research. In E. Sherman & W. Reid (Eds.), *Qualitative research in social work* (pp. 1-15). New York: Columbia University Press.

Spakes, P. & Nichols-Casebolt, A. (1994). Perspectives of women on family and social policy. *Affilia: Journal of Women and Social Work, 9* (4), 360-381.

Strauss, A. & Corbin, J. (1990). *Basics of qualitative research: Grounded theory procedures and techniques.* Newbury Park, CA: Sage Publications.

Thomas, S.L. (1995). Exchanging welfare checks for wedding rings: Welfare reform in New Jersey and Wisconsin. *Affilia: Journal of Women and Social Work, 10* (2), 120-137.

Toseland, R.W. (1994). Commentary: The qualitative/quantitative debate: Moving beyond acrimony to meaningful dialogue. In E. Sherman & W. Reid (Eds.), *Qualitative research in social work* (pp. 452-455). New York: Columbia University Press.

Women's Development Institute. (1995). *AFDC Parent Survey: Preliminary tabulations.* Augusta, ME: Author.

Work Opportunities Committee. (1981). *Women, work, and welfare.* Augusta, ME: Department of Human Services.

AFDC Recipients
and Family Caregiving Responsibilities

Sue J. Steiner

SUMMARY. This article explores the relationship between family caregiving among AFDC recipients and the length of time women remain on AFDC. Findings demonstrate a relationship between the poor health of children and the length of time a woman remains on AFDC, and provide a basis for suggesting two types of policy initiatives. First, AFDC recipients who have caregiving responsibilities for sick or disabled children should either be allowed to continue receiving public assistance to support their caregiving activities, or the state should provide alternative care options. Second, programs such as universal immunizations for children and universal health care that could improve the health of the poor, and thus alleviate some of the need for family caregiving by AFDC recipients, should be instituted. *[Article copies available for a fee from The Haworth Document Delivery Service: 1-800-342-9678. E-mail address: getinfo@haworth.com]*

KEYWORDS. Caregiving, AFDC, welfare, women, welfare reform

INTRODUCTION

As a society, we have harbored ambivalence about women's roles. We have been clear about the fact that women should take primary responsi-

Sue J. Steiner, PhD, is Assistant Professor, School of Social Work, Arizona State University, Box 871802, Tempe, AZ 85287-1802.

[Haworth co-indexing entry note]: "AFDC Recipients and Family Caregiving Responsibilities." Steiner, Sue J. Co-published simultaneously in *Journal of Poverty* (The Haworth Press, Inc.) Vol. 1, No. 2, 1997, pp. 63-79; and: *Income Security and Public Assistance for Women and Children* (ed: Keith M. Kilty, Virginia E. Richardson, and Elizabeth A. Segal) The Haworth Press, Inc., 1997, pp. 63-79. Single or multiple copies of this article are available for a fee from The Haworth Document Delivery Service [1-800-342-9678, 9:00 a.m. - 5:00 p.m. (EST). E-mail address: getinfo@haworth.com].

bility in the domestic/private sphere. We have been less sure of women's role in providing for the economic well-being of their families, and what should be done for women who have no man to provide for them. Some women have always been expected to work to support themselves and their families. Other women have warranted state support. The determination of which category a woman falls into has primarily been drawn along ethnic and racial lines, as well as whether or not a woman complies with proper sexual/childbearing behavior. White women and widows were more likely to receive state support than were women of color and women who bore children out of wedlock (Abramovitz, 1988).

Our societal ambivalence has spawned inconsistent and confusing social welfare policies. While we have provided assistance to some women and their families, we have done so reluctantly and with great debate about the merits and harms of providing aid. This confusion has increased in recent decades for a number of reasons. First, increases in divorce and nonmarital childbearing have meant a sharp rise in female-headed households (Ellwood, 1986). This means that there is no longer a male to go out and earn income to support the family while the woman takes care of the house and children. A second factor is the dramatic increase in female labor force participation. More American women are now working outside the home than at any other time in United States history. Over 60% of all women are in the paid labor force today compared with only 19% in the late 1880s (Goldin, 1990) and 35% as recently as 1960 (Fuchs, 1988). Particularly important to the welfare reform debate is the fact that almost 60% of women with children under two years old are now working outside the home. Increasingly the public is not only accepting working mothers, but expecting mothers, even those with young children, to work.

Even though women are entering the labor market at ever increasing rates, they still take primary responsibility for unpaid work around the house (Hartmann, 1987; Stetson, 1991). Additionally, women provide the vast majority of care for family members in need. Women constitute 72% of all family caregivers, and 77% of adult children providing care to aging parents (Abel, 1991). The intersection of women's roles as homemaker/caregiver and breadwinner creates a number of problems for women, their families, and society. These dual roles place a heavy and sometimes nearly impossible burden on women. Responsibilities for home and family interfere with a woman's ability to find and keep work, and to earn a living wage. Work in the labor force means that a woman has less time at home to provide care. This may mean that family members have unmet needs.

More likely it means that women work long hours to fulfill their many roles.

When we add poverty to the intersection of women's roles as caregiver and breadwinner, new problems surface. By definition, poor women have fewer financial resources available to them. Consequently, they have a greater need to work to provide for their families, and are less likely to be able to purchase any type of support services. Because poverty increases the likelihood of poor health or disability (Antonovsky, 1967; Freeman, 1989; Sardell, 1991), and poor health or disability can lead to poverty, it seems probable that there is an increased need for caregiving within poor families. This means that poor women may be called upon to provide care for sick or disabled family members quite often, and have little resources available to help them with their tasks.

The Aid to Families with Dependent Children (AFDC) program provides assistance to people who are among the poorest in society. Because most of the recipients are women, and women provide the vast majority of caregiving in this society, it seems likely that some of the women in this program are in a position of providing care for family members. Increasingly, pressure is being put on these women to leave AFDC and find jobs to support themselves and their families. This pressure can be seen in calls for welfare reform aimed at decreasing the size of the welfare rolls. Current suggestions for reform include limiting the time that people can receive AFDC, mandatory work programs, cutting benefits, and dismantling the system completely and putting children of low-income mothers into orphanages.

This paper will explore the issue of family caregiving among AFDC recipients, and its relationship to the length of time women remain on AFDC. Because it has been researched thoroughly elsewhere (Polit & O'Hara, 1989; Presser & Baldwin, 1980), the issue of providing care for healthy children will not be addressed. Caregiving here means the responsibility for providing care for family members in poor mental, emotional, or physical health. Findings from the study can contribute to the development of a humane and practical social welfare policy that addresses women's multiple roles.

METHODS

This study begins the task of exploring the relationship between the necessity of women to provide care for sick or disabled relatives and their status as recipients of AFDC by addressing the following research questions:

1. Is there a relationship between family caregiving responsibilities and the length of time a person remains on AFDC?
2. Can the number of months a person remains on public assistance be predicted by whether or not there is a sick family member in the household?

The study uses data gathered as part of a five-year longitudinal panel study called the Family Income Study (FIS). The study was commissioned by the Washington State Legislature in 1987. Its purpose was to conduct a longitudinal study of a sample of public assistance recipients or people at risk of becoming eligible for assistance, to try to determine the causes of public dependency. It was also designed to evaluate the Family Independence Program (FIP), which is a Washington State welfare reform project that provided cash assistance and other programs to a portion of the state's welfare population for a five year period that ended in July 1993.

SAMPLE

Respondents for the Family Income Study represent probability samples from one of two populations: (1) people already on public assistance, either AFDC or FIP, and (2) those at risk of public assistance. The at-risk group consists of members of the general population that live in areas with high concentrations of welfare use. For the purposes of the current research, a subsample of the total FIS sample was chosen for analysis. The subsample selected was composed of women from both the AFDC and at-risk populations who received public assistance from either the AFDC or FIP programs for at least one month over the five year period and who completed all five years of the study.

Sample Demographics

The demographics of the survey respondents used in this analysis can be seen in Table 1. The typical person in the sample was 30 years old, white, divorced, had two children, was the only adult in the household, and had not completed high school.

QUESTIONNAIRE AND VARIABLES

The Family Income Study questionnaire addressed questions about respondents' income and the source of all household income. It requested

TABLE 1. Demographic Characteristics of Public Assistance Recipients in Sample–Year 1

Median Age	30
Race	
White	80.4%
African American	5.2%
Native American	5.7%
Asian American/Pacific Islander	2.4%
Other Race	5.6%
Mixed Race	0.1%
Hispanic (any race)	5.6%
Marital Status	
Married	16.7%
Separated	14.5%
Divorced	36.8%
Widowed	1.8%
Never Married	30.3%
Average Number of Children	2
Only Adult in Household	58%
Education	
Not Complete High School	42%
High School Graduate	34%
GED	17%
2 or 4 Year College Degree	5%

N = 911

information on AFDC, FIP, Food Stamp, General Assistance, and Unemployment Compensation history, and included questions about why people originally started receiving these benefits. It also explored current employment status, and asked if people who were currently unemployed were looking for work, and if not, why not. The survey assessed in depth the physical health of the respondent and of any children in the household. It asked if there were any adults in the household whose poor health limited their ability to work or prevented them from working altogether. Finally, respondents answered numerous questions designed to assess their states of mental and emotional health, and levels of social support.

Respondents were not asked questions specifically about caregiving responsibilities. For the present study, a number of the variables described above were instead used to create a proxy measure for the variable of caregiving. Specifically, the measures described below were used to infer the presence of family caregiving responsibilities.

There were four measures of children's health:

1. Number of hospitalizations per child per year.
2. Number of acute illnesses per child per year.
3. Number of trips to the emergency room per child per year.
4. Whether or not each child had a chronic illness in a given year.

There were two measures of adult health:

1. Are there any adults in the household other than the respondent who have a mental, emotional or physical health problem that limits their ability to work?
2. Are there any adults in the household other than the respondent who have a mental, emotional, or physical health problem that prevents them from working?

Respondents were asked their reasons for first going on AFDC, and which reason was the most important. Finally, respondents who were not working and not looking for work gave reasons why they were not looking, including the most important reason. Choices for both of these questions included poor health of family members.

A number of variables were also used as control measures so that a more accurate picture of the effect of the proxy caregiving variables could be assessed. These variables include marital status, age, race, number of children in the household, education and previous work experience. Previous research has indicated a relationship between each of these variables and a person's AFDC status (Bane & Ellwood, 1983; Ellwood, 1986; Moffitt, 1992).

A variety of bivariate analyses were used to examine the strength of the association between the length of time on AFDC and various aspects of family health. These analyses consisted of chi-square tests and correlation techniques. Results from these procedures provided information to assist in model building for multivariate analyses. Standard and hierarchical multiple regression techniques were employed to assess the relationship between the predictive variables and the length of time on AFDC.

Analysis of longitudinal event data, such as the length of time a person remains on welfare, faces the problem of censoring or truncation of data. This study examined the length of time subjects received AFDC over a five year period, with specific beginning and end points. Because all of the subjects did not first receive AFDC when the study started, nor end their stay on welfare when the study ended, it was not possible to determine the actual length of their current AFDC spell. This poses a serious problem for the researcher who is interested in using the findings from a regression analysis to develop a simulation model, or estimating the effects of variables over the length of a given spell. As this study does not develop such a model or examine welfare spells, the use of standard regression is an appropriate analysis technique.

FINDINGS

The results of a number of bivariate analyses examining the relationships between the number of months on AFDC and the various proxy caregiving variables can be found in Table 2. In terms of the child health variables, a statistically significant relationship was found between the number of trips to the emergency room due to illness, number of acute illnesses, and whether or not a child had a chronic illness and the number of months they remained on AFDC. There was no significant relationship between the number of children's hospitalizations and number of months on AFDC.

No statistically significant relationship was found between whether or not there were sick adults other than the respondent in the household and the

TABLE 2. Summary of Bivariate Relationships Between Length of Time on AFDC and Health-Related Variables

Number of Months on AFDC by

Number of Times Children Hospitalized	$r = .07$
Number of Times Children to Emergency Room	$r = .17^{**}$
Number of Children's Acute Illnesses	$r = .19^{**}$

Long-term (more than 36 months) vs. Short-term AFDC by

Total Children's Illnesses, scale 1-4	$x^2 = 11.58^*$
Yes/No Child with Chronic Illness	$x^2 = 9.86^*$
Yes/No Sick or Disabled Adult	$x^2 = 0.10$
Reason on AFDC – Family Illness	$x^2 = 0.01$
Not Looking for Work – Family Illness	$x^2 = 1.23$

$n = 911$

* $= p < 0.05$

** $= p < 0.01$

r (Pearson Correlation Coefficient) was calculated when both variables were treated as continuous.

X^2 (Chi square) was calculated when both variables were treated as nominal or ordinal.

number of months on welfare. Nor was a significant relationship found between the length of time on AFDC and family illness as a reason for beginning to receive assistance or family illness as a reason for not looking for work.

Table 3 presents the results of a standard multivariate regression analysis with number of months on AFDC as the dependent variable. All of the proxy measures of caregiving are included as independent variables, as are a number of control variables. As stated earlier, each of the control variables has been found to have a relationship with a person's AFDC status in previous research.

The Multiple R for the equation is .37, and the Adjusted R Squared is .12. The adjusted R Squared, while significant, is relatively low; the model explains only 12 percent of the variation in number of months that a person remains on public assistance. Three of the control variables show statistical significance in this model: whether a respondent was African American or not; years of education; and if a respondent was married. The former was positively related, and the latter two negatively related to the number of months on welfare.

Two of the proxy caregiving measures, number of trips to the emergency room for children's illnesses, and number of children's acute illnesses also proved statistically significant and positively related to the amount of time on public assistance. It is difficult to interpret why these two child health variables are significant, and the others are not. This is due in part to the difficulty of interpreting several of the child health variables. As stated earlier, many low-income people use the emergency room instead of a primary care physician. It is possible that number of trips to the emergency room tends to measure this phenomenon, rather than trips for true emergencies. If this is the case, both of the significant variables might measure acute, rather than chronic, problems. This would suggest that child health problems that come and go are more closely related to the amount of time a woman spends on AFDC than are chronic problems. However, the presence or absence of a child with a chronic illness may not have proven to be statistically significant in this model because of its broad definition, as discussed above. The inclusion of both minor and major illnesses may have watered the variable down so much that it was not particularly useful.

Table 4 shows the results of a hierarchical multiple regression where all of the control variables were entered first, in a single block, to reduce the "noise" that they cause. The caregiving variables were then entered in the second step to determine what, if anything, they add to the equation. The Multiple R changed from .30 to .37 and the Adjusted R Squared from .07

TABLE 3. Standard Multiple Regression Model of Factors Associated with Length of Time on AFDC or FIP

Dependent Variable = number of months on AFDC/FIP over 5 years

Variable	B	S.E.	Beta	T
Asian	1.59	6.08	.01	.26
Yes/No Family Member Illness Reason for Beginning AFDC	.87	2.46	.01	.36
# Trips to the Emergency Room for Child's Illness	5.02	1.80	.12	2.78**
Black	9.29	4.32	.11	2.15*
Native American	2.02	4.00	.03	.50
Respondent Disabled	2.76	1.89	.06	1.46
Yes/No Respondent Worked Prior to AFDC	− 1.06	1.59	.03	− .67
Yes/No Respondent's Parents Received AFDC	− 2.54	1.49	− .07	− 1.70
Yes/No Disabled Adult in the Household	.97	2.05	.02	.48
# of Children in Household	3.81	3.58	.05	1.06
Yes/No Respondent Married	− 10.20	2.11	− .19	− 4.83**
# of Times Children Hospitalized Over 5 Years	− 1.28	2.20	− .02	− .58
Yes/No Child with Chronic Illness in the Household	− 1.09	1.59	− .03	− .69
Education Level of Respondent	− .90	.33	− .11	− 2.71**
# of Children's Acute Illnesses Over 5 Years	7.92	2.42	.15	3.27**
Respondent's Age	1.09	.12	.01	.01
White	.25	3.06	.01	.08
Constant	44.64	6.51		

n = 911
Multiple R = .37
Adjusted R Square = .12
F = 5.74   Signif F = .0000
(p < .05) *
(p < .01) **

TABLE 4. Hierarchical Regression Model of Factors Associated with Length of Time on AFDC or FIP

Dependent Variable = number of months on AFDC/FIP over 5 years

Variable	Variables Entered First Step		Variables Entered Second Step	
	B	S.E.	B	S.E.
Respondent Disabled	2.91	1.92	2.76	1.89
Native American	.45	4.05	2.02	4.00
Yes/No Respondent Worked Prior to AFDC	−1.25	1.61	−1.06	1.59
Black	7.25	4.37	9.29*	4.32
Respondent's Age	−.21	.11	−.04	.09
Asian	2.68	6.16	1.59	6.08
Yes/No Respondent Married	−10.58**	2.06	−10.20**	2.11
Yes/No Respondent's Parents Received AFDC	−2.54	1.52	−2.54	1.49
Education Level of Respondent	.83**	.34	−.90**	.33
# Children in the Household	8.97**	3.47	3.81	3.58
White	−.42	3.08	.25	3.06
# of Times Children Hospitalized Over 5 Years			−1.28	2.20
Yes/No Family Member Illness Reason for Beginning AFDC			.88	2.46
Yes/No Child with Chronic Illness in the Household			−1.09	1.59
Yes/No Disabled Adult in the Household			.97	2.05
# Trips to the Emergency Room for Child's Illness			5.02**	1.80
# of Children's Acute Illnesses Over 5 Years			7. 92**	2.42
Constant	61.75	5.23	44.64	6.51

n = 911
Multiple R = .37
Adjusted R Square = .11
R Square Change = .05
F change = 5.61   Signif F Change = .0000
F = 5.74   Signif F = .0000
(p < .05)*
(p < .01) * *

to .11 with the addition of the caregiving variables. The R Squared Change is .05, which is statistically significant at the .001 level. This means that the inclusion of the proxy caregiving variables does add to the predictive ability of the overall equation.

DISCUSSION

A number of the results suggest that there is a relationship between some family health variables and a woman's AFDC or FIP status. One of the descriptive statistics suggests such a relationship. Eighty-eight respondents, which constitutes 9.7% of those who received AFDC or FIP over the five year period, cited the presence of mentally or physically ill children or adults as the reason why they initially went on welfare. If that figure were translated to a state level it would mean that caregiving responsibilities were a precipitating factor in the need for AFDC for over 9,000 people in Washington state in a year.

A relationship between family health and the length of time a recipient remains on AFDC can also be seen in a number of the bivariate and regression analyses. This relationship was particularly clear with the children's health variables. Three of the four child health variables proved to be significantly and positively related to length of time on public assistance in the bivariate analyses. Moreover, number of trips to the emergency room for children's illnesses and number of children's acute illnesses were two of only five variables that were consistently significant in the regression analyses. Put simply, this means that the higher the number of acute illnesses or trips to the emergency room, the more months a woman will tend to receive AFDC.

Both of the regression models used produced relatively small Adjusted R Squared statistics, which means that they are of limited use in explaining the variation in length of time that respondents remain on AFDC. Similarly, while a number of variables were statistically significantly correlated with the variable for number of months on public assistance, the magnitude of the correlations was small. Both of these may be due to the fact that the reasons a person remains on public assistance are quite complex, and frequently difficult to determine. However, it is clear that the addition of at least several of the child health variables as part of the hierarchical regression analysis, adds to the quality of the regression equation. Their addition seems to be one step in improving our understanding of long-term welfare use.

The variables used to infer respondent caregiving responsibilities for sick adults, as compared with sick children, did not prove to be related to amount of time on public assistance, and were not clearly useful in improving the regression equation. This may mean that the poor health of adult household members is not related to how long a person receives assistance. It is possible that the relatively young age of most welfare recipients means that they do not yet have a responsibility for caring for aging parents, or other relatives. It may, however, mean instead that the variables used to measure the poor health of adults other than the respondent were inadequate. This issue will be discussed in more depth in the next section.

It should be noted once again that this study only examines women who received AFDC or FIP for at least one month over a five year period. It looks at the number of months that people received assistance, given that they did receive assistance. This research does not examine the issue of why women go on welfare, but rather, what factors are related to the amount of time that they remain on public assistance. Factors that influence the former, may be quite different from those that affect the latter.

IMPLICATIONS FOR POLICY AND PRACTICE

Policy Implications

The results from this study suggest two broad types of policy initiatives. The first addresses changes in AFDC related policies. As stated above, children's health variables appear to be among the strongest predictors of length of time women remain on welfare. *This suggests that some women are not able to work enough in the labor market to provide for their families at least in part due to the fact that they must care for children in poor health.* Attempts at welfare reform that force all able-bodied women off welfare through mandatory work programs and limits on welfare duration, would need to insure alternative caregiving arrangements, or allow some exceptions related to other family members' health.

This country is currently struggling with the question of what is the most cost effective and humane way to provide long-term care for all those who cannot care for themselves. Care provided by relatives is currently the cheapest alternative. If the poor are at increased risk for illness and disability, as a large amount of research indicates, families supported by public assistance may have a great need for both short-term and long-term care. Thus, recipients who are providing this care in exchange for the small amount of money they receive in the form of AFDC benefits, may provide the most cost effective solution to this problem. If women on welfare are forced to enter the labor market and are no longer available to provide care, a more expensive alternative will need to be found.

One policy alternative that would be cost effective under these circumstances would be for women who are primary care providers for relatives who cannot care for themselves to be exempt from mandatory work programs and from regulations stipulating an upper limit on welfare duration. Women who are providing ongoing care are doing a job that someone else would have to be paid for, and that others are already being paid for when no family is available to provide care (although usually not paid nearly enough). Thus, they could be exempt with the understanding that they are already working.

A more humane expansion of this policy would allow women a choice as to whether they wanted to remain at home and provide care, or have other care available so that they could work outside the home with the knowledge that their relatives were receiving quality care. However, in a time of tight budgets, this alternative is likely to be only remotely possible if long-term care is included in the health care reform package.

The problem is somewhat more complicated for situations where a relative does not need ongoing, long-term care, but rather periodic care. This might be the case with a child who has frequent, acute illnesses that keep her or him out of school or day care. In these situations, the woman is not needed all of the time to provide care, yet the times when she is needed may disrupt her work and/or cause her to lose jobs. While there do not seem to be any easy solutions to this problem, a number of policies could be instituted to begin to address the problem.

First, additional money for care of sick children could be provided as part of child care subsidies in welfare reform packages to pay for in-home sick child care on days when children are too sick to attend school or day care. Unfortunately, in a time of shrinking rather than expanding benefits, there is probably little political future in this. If we truly believe that it is better for all poor women to work outside the home than be supported by the government, a second option is to adopt a policy where the government would supplement a woman's salary on days that she is not at work because she must provide care for sick family members. An expanded family leave policy would be needed in conjunction with this to insure that women would not lose their jobs for time at home with family members who need care. A third option is to accept the fact that some women with children will not be able to work because of intermittent health problems that their children may have, and allow these women to remain on AFDC until they are no longer needed at home.

In addition to allowing women who have caregiving responsibilities to remain at home and receive benefits, a truly progressive policy would actually raise benefit levels for these women. As discussed earlier, the provision of care is often expensive. Moreover, the women who are performing these caregiving duties are probably saving the state from having to pay more for some other type of services. One way of approaching such a policy would be to set benefit and eligibility levels higher for families with a sick family member. For example, the sick person could be counted as two people, so that a family of four would receive the benefits normally given to a family of five. While such a policy would increase current welfare costs, it would, in all likelihood, be less expensive than providing other types of long or short-term care.

The second general policy approach comes at the issue from the other side: by reducing the need for caregiving. If sick children are a factor in the length of time that women remain on AFDC, one way to reduce the problem is to improve the health of poor children. Many childhood illnesses and disabilities are preventable (Sardell, 1991). Policies that support prevention, such as increased prenatal care and immunizations for all children, could go a long way in reducing childhood illnesses and thus the need for provision of care. These programs are also potentially politically feasible, because they can be shown to be cost effective in the long run. A relatively small amount of money spent on prenatal care and immunizations now can save us from spending large amounts in the future to treat and provide care for conditions that could have been prevented.

Universal health insurance will also likely reduce health problems among the poor, and thus reduce the need for caregiving. While those on AFDC currently receive health insurance through Medicaid, lack of universal health insurance probably increases the amount of illness among families on AFDC. This is true because many of those who are currently poor, yet not receiving AFDC and thus not eligible for Medicaid, may be receiving AFDC at some time in the future. Many among this group are likely to be uninsured. Currently, between 32 and 38 million Americans, a large percentage of whom are children, have no health insurance. Of these, roughly 20 million live above the poverty line, and 17 million live below the poverty level. This means that about half of the nation's 34 million people living below the poverty line are too rich for Medicaid, yet too poor to afford other insurance (Freeman, 1989).

Poor health may cause many members of this group to resort to public assistance to support their families. Poor health is cited by 7.8% of the FIS respondents as the most important reason why they initially went on AFDC. This is probably the case both because women were sick and could not work, and because some had to spend all that they had to cover medical expenses, and were thus left with no alternative but to be supported through public assistance. Additionally, women who were able to get off AFDC and go to work, commonly cite poor health as a reason why they were forced to leave jobs and return to public assistance.

Of those who begin to receive AFDC for reasons other than poor health, they or their family members may be in worse health while they are on public assistance due to lack of insurance prior to receiving AFDC. Research indicates that those without insurance and/or financial resources receive less preventative care, and thus suffer worse health problems than people with health insurance (Daniels, 1978; Hadley, Steinberg & Feder, 1991). Thus, comprehensive, universal health insurance appears to be another policy option that would improve the health of the poor, and thus reduce the need for caregiving by AFDC recipients.

Implications for Social Work Practice

In terms of social work practice, social workers must be aware that caregiving responsibilities may comprise a serious problem for women on welfare. If we are unable to change policy and create a situation that offers women on welfare realistic options, we must find ways to help these women cope with their situations. One basic option to explore is the creation of support networks or groups. Bringing women who share similar problems together can create needed social support, and may also create an environment where solutions to common problems can emerge.

Another possible approach is the creation of some type of cooperative arrangement between women who have caregiving responsibilities and are trying to work. If groups of women can find ways to share some of their caregiving tasks, this might be a way of opening up more time for the individual women involved. This type of solution would likely prove most useful in situations where caregiving responsibilities are relatively small and do not require large expenditures of time. This is most likely in cases where the illness or disability is not so severe as to require constant attention from the caregiver.

Community organizing and/or labor organizing may also be used to address some of the issues that this population faces. Because caregiving responsibilities are problematic for women at all socioeconomic levels, community and labor organizing can bring divergent groups of women together to try to develop programs and policies that will address their common needs. Organizing efforts could target such communities as welfare recipients, low-wage women employees, all women employees, and/or parents of disabled children, to name just a few.

Community education, and consciousness raising can also be employed as change tactics. A first step to creating real change for low income caregivers is for policy makers and the general population to begin to address the inherent contradiction in our multiple expectations of the roles that women should fill. While some women can work enough to support themselves and their families, and take care of the house and all of its inhabitants, few women can do this without great personal cost. The situation is particularly difficult for the poor, who lack outside resources to assist them. Community education and consciousness raising can be employed to dispel the expectation that women can and should do it all.

This research raises many difficult issues that are central to our beliefs and value systems. Implementation of both the policy and practice recommendations discussed above will mean addressing some of the sexism inherent in both the welfare system and the labor market. It will require a rethinking of our assumptions regarding women's roles, and a realistic examination of the impact that a change in those roles has had on women, and on society as a whole. It will also demand a critical evaluation of the belief that the optimal goal of welfare reform is an end to welfare dependence for all women. The result of this reevaluation may be the realization that women who care for sick family members are "working women," and are providing a valuable service for which they should be adequately compensated. If women have no other source of support, that compensation should come from the state.

REFERENCES

Abel, E.K. (1991). *Who cares for the elderly: Public policy and the experiences of adult daughters.* Philadelphia: Temple University Press.

Abramovitz, M. (1988). *Regulating the lives of women: Social welfare policy from colonial times to the present.* Boston: South End Press.

Antonovsky, A. (1967). Social class, life expectancy, and overall mortality. *Milbank Memorial Fund Quarterly, 45,* 37-73.

Bane, M.J., & Ellwood, D. (1983). The dynamics of dependence: The routes to self-sufficiency. Report for the Office of Income Security Policy. Washington, DC: Department of Health and Human Services.

Daniels, N. (1978). *Just health care.* Cambridge, MA: Harvard University Press.

Ellwood, D. (1986). Targeting 'would be' long-term recipients of AFDC. Princeton, NJ: Mathematica Policy Research.

Freeman, H.P. (1989). Cancer in the economically disadvantaged. *Cancer, 64*(1), 324-334.

Fuchs, V.R. (1988). *Women's quest for economic equality.* Cambridge, MA: Harvard University Press.

Goldin, C. (1990). *Understanding the gender gap: An economic history of American women.* New York: Oxford University Press.

Hadley, J., Steinberg, E.P., Feder, J. (1991). Comparison of uninsured and privately insured hospital patients. *Journal of the American Medical Association,* 265(3), 374-379.

Hartmann, H. (1987). Internal labor markets and gender: A case study of promotion. In C. Brown & J. Pechman (Eds.), *Gender in the work place.* Washington, DC: The Brookings Institute.

Moffitt, R. (1992). Incentive effects of the U.S. welfare system: A review. *Journal of Economic Literature, 30,* 1-61.

Presser, H., & Baldwin, W. (1980). Child care as a constraint on employment: Prevalence, correlates, and bearing on the work and fertility nexus. *American Journal of Sociology, 85,* 1202-1213.

Sardell, A. (1991). Child health policy in the U.S.: The paradox of consensus. In L.D. Brown (Ed.), *Health policy and the disadvantaged* (pp. 17-53). Durham: Duke University Press.

Stetson, D.M. (1991). *Women's rights in the U.S.A.: Policy debates and gender roles.* Pacific Grove, CA: Cole Publishing.

Poverty and Child Placement:
A New/Old Idea

Nora S. Gustavsson
Ann E. MacEachron

SUMMARY. One result of the Republican victories in November 1994 is the suggestion that the children of the poor should be separated from their parents. The removal of children for no other reason than poverty is an old idea. The article examines the historical precedents of child placement, reviews the experience of the poorest group of Americans (Native Americans) and analyzes child placement through the lens of poverty. In addition, the role of the federal government in protecting vulnerable children is examined by comparing two federal laws–the Indian Child Welfare Act and the Adoption Assistance and Child Welfare Act. *[Article copies available for a fee from The Haworth Document Delivery Service: 1-800-342-9678. E-mail address: getinfo@haworth.com]*

KEYWORDS. Poverty, child placement, family separation, Native Americans, vulnerability, public policy, punitive, out-of-home placement, institutionalization

One consequence of the conservative Republican victories in the general elections of November 1994 has been the reemergence of public

Nora S. Gustavsson, PhD, is Associate Professor, School of Social Work, Arizona State University, Tempe, AZ 85287-1802.

Ann E. MacEachron, PhD, is Professor, School of Social Work, Arizona State University, Tempe, AZ 85287-1802.

[Haworth co-indexing entry note]: "Poverty and Child Placement: A New/Old Idea." Gustavsson, Nora S., and Ann E. MacEachron. Co-published simultaneously in *Journal of Poverty* (The Haworth Press, Inc.) Vol. 1, No. 2, 1997, pp. 81-93; and: *Income Security and Public Assistance for Women and Children* (ed: Keith M. Kilty, Virginia E. Richardson, and Elizabeth A. Segal) The Haworth Press, Inc., 1997, pp. 81-93. Single or multiple copies of this article are available for a fee from The Haworth Document Delivery Service [1-800-342-9678, 9:00 a.m. - 5:00 p.m. (EST). E-mail address: getinfo@haworth.com].

policy discussions that are premised on antiquated and punitive notions about the poor. Our first purpose, through a brief historical analysis, is to reveal the lack of originality of the current Republican proposal that institutional care for dependent children is an innovative and potentially effective public policy in child welfare. Our second purpose is to highlight the unfortunately intimate connection between poverty and out-of-home placement among the historically oppressed Native Americans. Here we discuss the Indian Child Welfare Act of 1978 which has the mission to break this connection. A related purpose is to compare the current Native American experience in helping vulnerable children with our national experience since the landmark child welfare legislation passed in 1980, the Adoption Assistance and Child Welfare Act.

A common legislative intent of both Acts is to reduce the number and percent of children in out-of-home placements, although only the Indian Child Welfare Act emphasizes societal oppression against the poor and culturally different as main reasons for out-of-home placements. Analysis of placement rates occurring before and after the passage of both Acts suggests, however, that placement is an ineffectual method for dealing with poverty and that other federal actions are more likely to accomplish such social goals as the reduction of poverty.

POVERTY AND INSTITUTIONAL ARRANGEMENTS FOR CHILDREN

Poverty has been a community if not societal concern since the inception of the American republic. A review of colonial era documents reveals a rather consistent theme regarding the dread of poverty among communities (Pumphrey & Pumphrey, 1961). The origin of this fear is subject to interpretation; however, it seems clear from an economic perspective that survival was the major concern of most colonists. Although wealth existed in colonial America it was primarily an agrarian wealth of owning land rather than an owning of capital per se; thus wealth as it is understood today was rare in colonial America. More importantly, however, this form of wealth limited the ability of communities to support non-contributing (as defined by the elites) or poor members.

The body politic often interpreted political (e.g., individualism) and religious (e.g., Protestant Ethic) beliefs as being congruent with such economic realities. Methods for caring for the dependent also reflected such economic realities and included outdoor relief (primarily in-kind provision of food and fuel), indenture, and farming out (Kadushin & Martin, 1988). But not all methods for caring were consistent with the agrarian economic structure. The colonists, for example, imported the principles of the Elizabethan Poor Law of 1601 and the Settlement Act of 1662 even though conditions in England which led to these acts and those in Colonial America were vastly different. It was illogical if not counterproductive, for instance, for communities to require poor people and others in need to remain in the community to be eligible for whatever meager assistance the community was willing to provide when economic opportunity in the form of land was available outside the community. Indeed, availability of vast natural resources, expansionism, and belief in the expendability of the indigenous Native American populations combined ultimately to encourage a westward movement of the population in general.

Institutions, as a method of caring, did not flourish until the 1800s. From their inception to the early 20th century, most institutions were run by religious groups with limited funds from the public treasury. These institutions housed many types of dependents. Orphaned children, people with physical, emotional, and mental disabilities, the alcohol dependent, delinquent, and poor populated the alms house in the early part of the 19th century. However, infant mortality rates due to infectious diseases combined with poor hygiene and nutrition were high and could exceed 90% (Costin, Bell & Downs, 1991). Institutional reform activities began to take shape by the mid-1800s and accelerated after the Civil War. Among the major reforms promulgated were efforts to separate children from the general institutional population and to find alternative living arrangements for children. By the end of the 19th century, there were also reform attempts to separate young offenders from adults. Public, rather than private, institutional care for children, delinquents, and economically marginal adults had also become a well-established practice by the 20th century.

An alternative to the aggregate, institutional care of children was formalized in the mid-19th century but did not flourish until the late 20th century. Foster care began as an attempt to "save" children from the evils of their poor, urban-dwelling, immigrant parents. The Reverend Mr. Charles Loring Brace, founder of the Children's Aid Society, is credited with articulating this philosophy and with the establishment of foster care as a method of child saving (Brace, 1872). Beginning in 1853 Brace gathered children from areas of New York City which housed recent immigrants. For unstated and undocumented reasons, Brace and others assumed that these children were orphaned or abandoned. The children were placed on trains and sent to the Midwest where farm families agreed to provide care for the youngsters. Little was known about the people caring for these children since there was no social investigation. The exact nature of this care is subject to question; but nonetheless, in a 76-year period, more than 31,000 children were placed (Thurston, 1930).

It was not until the Progressive Era that serious reform efforts came to fruition. The wanton destruction of families for reasons of poverty was beginning to be viewed as unacceptable. The great reformers of the early 20th century such as Jane Addams, Grace and Edith Abbott, Julia Lathrop, Florence Kelly and others played a major role in creating and mobilizing the forces necessary to convince the political elites that the federal government had a responsibility to children. One result of these efforts was the first White House Conference on Dependent Children in 1909. This watershed event led to major reforms including the mandate to establish the first federal agency concerned with children—the Children's Bureau in 1912. Another contribution of the conference was the policy position that poverty was an insufficient reason for disrupting families. "Except in unusual circumstances, the home should not be broken up for reasons of poverty" (Proceedings, 1909, p. 10).

However, translating this important axiom—of not placing children due to family poverty—into practice had been fraught with challenges. In the child welfare arena, the rates of reported maltreatment suggest that poverty has been reframed from being a lack of material resources to being miscreant behavior perpetrated by incompetent parents upon their children. Maltreatment that is reported to authorities is seven times more likely to occur in poor families than in non-poor families, making family income a predictor of maltreatment (U.S. Department of Health and Human Services, 1988). Indeed, parents, in contemporary America and including the last half of the 20th century, may lose custody of their children because of medical and educational neglect and what is euphemistically termed environmental neglect: inadequate housing, lack of working plumbing, or the presence of health or fire hazards in the home. All these conditions are frequently associated with poverty, and some of the increase in the foster care population which occurred in the late 1980s and early 1990s has been attributed to an increase in the number of children and families living in poverty (General Accounting Office, 1995). In the following sections we discuss the relationship between poverty and out-of-home placement of children in terms of the apparent influence of the Indian Child Welfare Act of 1978 and the Adoption Assistance and Child Welfare Act of 1980.

NATIVE AMERICAN CHILD WELFARE

Native Americans have been subject to a number of policies which have threatened the very survival of this indigenous population (Hull,

1982). Policies have ranged from extermination to assimilation (Blanchard, 1987; Danzinger, 1991; Prucha, 1985). However, poverty has been used as the primary weapon and excuse to destroy Native American Families.

Indian children were subject to the institutionalization movement that characterized 19th century America. The Native American version of the institution was the boarding school. The schools served to "civilize" the children. Thousands of children were placed in these schools (Prucha, 1990). The purpose of the schools was to sever children from their culture. In many instances, Indian children were required to speak English only; their names were changed to conventional English names; they were not permitted to practice their religion but were taught Christianity; and they were not allowed to return to their homes (Indian Education, 1969).

As federal policy towards Native Americans vacillated, institutional arrangements for the children changed. Nevertheless, attempts to save Indian children from their families did not falter. Government as well as social welfare organizations such as the Child Welfare League of America combined their talents and instituted wholesale adoption programs in which the overwhelming majority of the children were adopted by non-Indians (Davies, 1982; Lyslo, 1967). Few of the children adopted were orphans. Most had parents, but their parents were poor.

Placement rates for Indian children were the highest for any group of America's children. Indian children were placed at rates more than twenty times higher than that of white children (Johnson, 1981). The national overall placement rate for children in the early 1970s was approximately one out of two hundred. In North and South Dakota and Nebraska, one out of every nine Indian children were not in their homes with their parents but were in placement with non-Indians (Baler, 1977; Scope of the problem, 1974). By the 1970s nearly 25% of Indian children were not living with their families (Johnson, 1981).

This extraordinary placement rate can be attributed to multiple variables. Discrimination and the imposition of white middle-class notions of family along with high rates of poverty combined to provide the fodder needed to sustain dependency petitions in many jurisdictions. Poverty has been and continues to be a pervasive problem in the Indian community (Dolgoff, Feldstein, & Skolnik, 1993). Thirty percent of Native American households live below the poverty level and in some urban areas, two thirds of Native American children live in poverty (Reddy, 1993).

FEDERAL CORRECTIVE ACTION

Eventually the Congress acted to stop the cultural genocide such widespread placement policy perpetuates and passed the Indian Child Welfare

Act of 1978, P.L. 95-608. The Act contained provisions to limit placement by requiring child welfare workers to demonstrate that services to keep the family together had not worked, and tribes were now to be involved and their consent was necessary for placement (both foster and adoptive). A particularly interesting section of the act restricted the ability of state courts to consider poverty as a reason to remove an Indian child. Again, the federal government formally recognized (as was the case in the 1909 White House Conference on Children) the questionable relationship between poverty and parental maltreatment of children.

The implementation of this Act has not been without controversy. For example, the supporters of transracial adoption are concerned that the line between the personal and the political may victimize children. Such an argument suggests that the overall goal of preserving cultural identity is noble but an individual child should not be denied a loving home just to meet political goals. The adoption standards of the Child Welfare League of America, for example, state that racial background should not determine the selection of a home and that children have a right to be adopted by families that are racially dissimilar (1968).

A commonly held cultural belief in the ineffectiveness of government, especially big government, began a rapid apogee during the Reagan era and may have reached its zenith in the Republican victories of 1994. However, a critical examination of the effectiveness of various federal programs, and social welfare programs in particular, suggests that there are, indeed, effective federal programs such as Headstart and prenatal and nutrition programs (Children's Defense Fund, 1989; Levitan, 1990). The Indian Child Welfare Act has been examined and results are encouraging. Data from a national survey indicate that placement rates have been declining (Plantz et al., 1989). Other data sources also show a decline in placement rates and a significant decrease in placement rates when compared with non-Indian children (Elbert, 1988; Tatara, 1988). A secondary analysis which looked at adoptive and foster care placement rates, and the incidence of cross-racial placement, indicated that there had been changes consistent with the intent of the Indian Child Welfare Act (MacEachron, 1992).

CONTEMPORARY PLACEMENT AND POOR CHILDREN

A few years after the passage of the Indian Child Welfare Act, the Congress enacted major legislation designed to reform public child welfare and provide vulnerable children with permanent living arrangements, preferably with their biological or adoptive families. The primary goals of the Adoption Assistance and Child Welfare Act of 1980, P.L. 96-272, included reducing the number of children entering foster care by forcing states to make reasonable efforts to prevent placement, requiring states to actively plan for the future of the children entering care (permanency planning), and facilitating adoption (Gustavsson & Segal, 1994). Prior to this legislation, large numbers of children had been in foster care for protracted periods, at costs which ran into the billions, and with little systematic planning for their future. These youngsters were at risk for growing up in a system in which they were likely to experience multiple placements with little opportunity for developing long lasting relationships with a caretaker.

The effectiveness of this legislation has yet to be determined. While there was an initial decline in the number of children in substitute care for a few years after the Act was implemented, it is unclear what factors accounted for the decline. During the mid-1970s the foster care population was estimated to be about a half million. It dropped in the early 1980s and began climbing in the mid-1980s. Between 1986 and 1989 the foster care population changed from 280,000 to 360,000, an increase of 29%. By 1992, the population reached 440,000, an increase of more than 50% since 1986 (Committee on Ways and Means, 1991; Pelton, 1993). Recently, the number of children in care has reached new levels. The foster care population reflects similar increases in the prison population (U.S. Department of Justice, 1994). Both are at new heights. It is interesting to note that, unlike the Indian Child Welfare Act, the Adoption Assistance and Child Welfare Act did not specify that poverty could not be used as the basis for removing children from their families.

The Adoption Assistance and Child Welfare Act did require states to make reasonable efforts to prevent placement. Reasonable efforts were not operationalized. Other child welfare legislation has addressed this issue. Family support and preservation legislation was codified as part of Title IV-B of the Social Security Act in 1993. Even this legislation does not require states to provide any specific actions or services. States are encouraged to develop programs which ensure the safety of family members and also strengthen families.

The characteristics of children entering care reinforce the view that public child welfare remains a residual social welfare service for poor children. There continues to be a strong correlation between parental poverty and child placement (General Accounting Office, 1995). It could be argued that the poor are more likely, due to stress and other environmental factors, to hurt their children than the non-poor. However, the majority of children enter care because of allegations of neglect, not physical or sexual abuse. Neglect remains the umbrella which communities can use to impose child rearing standards and living requirements on the recalcitrant poor. When these standards are not met, the poor may lose their children. This is a well-established American policy, dating back to the early days of the republic.

Minority children are especially vulnerable to both placement and poverty. One third of Hispanic children reared in female-headed families live in poverty, and 60% of African American children in female-headed households live in poverty (Gustavsson & Segal, 1994). African American children comprise almost half of the foster care population, enter care at a higher rate and are less likely to leave care than are white children (Committee on Ways and Means, 1991). A five-city study of African American children in care revealed that the majority were placed for neglect, almost two thirds came from families supported by AFDC, and their caretakers had numerous problems such as inadequate housing, drug abuse, and mental health problems (National Black Child Development Institute, 1989).

Drug use by women is blamed for much of the increase in child protective and foster care caseloads and serves to highlight the relationship between poverty and placement. The socially disapproved behaviors of women, particularly poor minority women, are reflected in child welfare policy and practice. During the 1980s, poor drug using women began to be viewed as the perpetrators of fetal abuse, and punitive policies of limited effectiveness were the response (Gustavsson, 1991). The women were subject to criminal prosecution, and their children could be removed from their custody for no reason other than the use of a chemical assumed to be harmful to the fetus.

Justification for this Draconian intervention is based on questionable assumptions. A critical review of the data reveals that a causal relationship between fetal harm and maternal illicit drug use needs further research and that some of the negative effects observed in some infants may attenuate with age (Chasnoff et al., 1992; Zuckerman & Frank, 1992). However, the evidence establishing an association between fetal harm and legal drugs such as alcohol and tobacco remains strong (Rosengren, 1990; Office on Smoking and Health, 1988; Streissguth, Sampson, & Barr, 1989). Legal drugs are used by large numbers of women, including white middle-class women.

Further, an examination of drug use patterns indicated that white women were in many cases more frequent users of drugs than African American women (National Institute of Drug Abuse, 1989). Studies which controlled for the effects of social class and race found that poor and

African American pregnant women were more likely to be referred to public child welfare agencies for alleged drug use than were non-poor and white women (Chasnoff, Landress, & Barrett, 1990). Nevertheless, the myth that drug use by minority women was at an all time high and was responsible for fetal harm became entrenched. One consequence was that the 1980s witnessed large numbers of very young children entering placement (Select Committee on Children, Youth & Families, 1989).

While more children are entering care, more families are being referred for child protective services. In 1992, child welfare agencies received almost 1.9 million reports alleging that 2.9 million children were victims of maltreatment. Less than half of the reports were substantiated. Neglect was the form of maltreatment in more than 50% of the substantiated reports (National Center on Child Abuse and Neglect, 1994). The resources of child welfare agencies are taxed by such a large demand for services, and in some areas the response of the agencies has been inadequate, resulting in litigation. Child welfare services by class action is a trend that was begun in the 1980s and is now firmly established. A number of states and jurisdictions (Illinois, District of Columbia, Baltimore, Arkansas, and Utah) have been sued for failing to provide required services or meet minimum requirements of the Adoption Assistance and Child Welfare Act (Angela R. v. Clinton, 1991; David C. et al. v. Leavitt, 1994; Suter v. Artist M., 1992; L.J. v. Massinga, 1989). The result of these neglectful actions by the state has been harm, and in some cases, death for children in the care of the state.

CONCLUSION

Current suggestions that public policy should be changed to encourage the separation of children from their families for no reason other than poverty is not new. Poverty and placement have been inextricably woven for hundreds of years. What is of concern is the amount of agreement such a policy initiative has garnered. While groups are forming to counter the myths about AFDC (Landers, 1995), there has been a notable lack of vigorous response from the child welfare industry. It is still early, and opposition to institutionalization may be in the formative stages.

Government can be an effective tool in preventing the destruction of poor families. The Indian Child Welfare Act, in spite of continuing implementation problems, not the least of which is a lack of resources so tribes can carry out the intent of the Act, has resulted in reduced placement rates for Native American children. Unfortunately, the Adoption Assistance and Child Welfare Act has not had the same outcome. A return to institutionalization or the forced separation of certain specific groups from the community began in the 1980s and shows little sign of abating in the 1990s. As a nation we are housing more and more of our fellow citizens in placements whether jails for adults or foster and group care for children. The United States established a record in 1993 when almost one million citizens were incarcerated, a 188% increase since 1980 (U.S. Department of Justice, 1994). The effectiveness of institutionalization will be questioned again. In the meantime, many children will once again face the risk of separation from their families for reasons of poverty alone.

The debates about welfare reform provide an opportunity to educate lawmakers as well as citizens about the dangers of poverty and the needs of children. Government programs can help vulnerable groups such as poor children. One strategy for countering the Republican attack on federal policy initiatives is to highlight the programs that have achieved success in a fiscally responsible manner.

Distortions about poor families (i.e., women have children in order to get AFDC) are harmful and can be countered with empirical data. Examples of programs that support families (family based services) and which are cost effective exist (General Accounting Office, 1993). In an era marked by great interest in saving tax money through reducing spending in the human service field, cost effectiveness can be used to engender support for policies and programs which focus on poor families. Highlighting the success of governmental policies runs counter to the political current in which government (especially the federal government) is viewed as abusive and ineffective. However, it is a necessary strategy if the cycle of family disruption due to poverty is to be disrupted.

REFERENCES

Angela R. v. Clinton, No. LR-C-91-415 (E.D. Ark, filed July 8, 1991).

Blanchard, E.L. (1987). American Indians and Alaska Natives. In A. Minahan (Ed.), *Encyclopedia of Social Work,* Vol. 1, (18th ed.), (pp. 142-150). Silver Springs, MD: National Association of Social Workers.

Brace, C.L. (1872). *The dangerous classes of New York and twenty years' work among them.* New York: Wynkoop & Hallenbeck.

Byler, W. (1977) The destruction of American Indian families. In S. Unger (Ed.), *The destruction of American Indian families* (pp. 1-11). New York: Association of American Indian Affairs.

Chasnoff, I., Griffith, D., Freier, C., & Murray, J. (1992). Cocaine/polydrug use in pregnancy: Two year follow-up. *Pediatrics, 89,* 284-289.

Chasnoff, I., Landress, H., & Barrett, M. (1990). The prevalence of illicit-drug or alcohol use during pregnancy and discrepancies in mandatory reporting in

Pinellas County, Florida. *New England Journal of Medicine, 322*(17), 1202-1206.

Child Welfare League of America. (1968). *Standards for adoption services (rev. ed)*. New York: Author.

Children's Defense Fund. (1989). *A vision for America's future*. Washington, DC: Author.

Committee on Ways and Means. (1991). *1991 green book. Background material and data on programs within the jurisdiction of the Committee on Ways and Means* (Committee Print 102-109). Washington, DC: U.S. Government Printing Office.

Costin, L.B., Bell, C.J., & Downs, S.W. (1991). *Child welfare policies and practice* (4th ed.). White Plains, NY: Longman.

Danzinger, E.J., Jr. (1991). *Survival and regeneration: Detroit's American Indian community*. Detroit: Wayne State University Press.

David C. v. Leavitt, et al, No. 93-C-206W (D. Utah, C.D. Order of Final Approval of Settlement Agreement, August 29, 1994). Clearinghouse No. 48,842.

Davies, B. (1982). Implementing the Indian Child Welfare Act. *Clearinghouse Review,* July 179-196.

Dolgoff, R., Feldstein, D., & Skolnik, L. (1993). *Understanding social welfare* (3rd ed.). White Plains, NY: Longman.

Elbert, H.E. (1988). State adoption reports pursuant to P.L. 95-608-Indian Child Welfare Act. Printed in U.S. Senate Hearing, To amend the Indian Child Welfare Act. *Hearing before the Select Committee on Indian Affairs, United States Senate, 100th Congress,* 2nd Sess., May11, pp. 56-57. Washington, DC: U.S. Government Printing Office.

Gustavsson, N.S. (1991). Pregnant chemically dependent women: The new criminals. *Affilia, 6*(2), 61-73.

Gustavsson, N.S. & Segal, E.A. (1994). *Critical issues in child welfare*. Newbury Park, CA: Sage.

Hull, G.H. Jr. (1982). Child welfare services to Native Americans. *Social Casework, (63)*6, 340-347.

Indian Education: A national tragedy: A national challenge. (1969). Washington, DC: Committee on Labor and Public Welfare, Special Subcommittee on Indian Education; U.S. Senate, 91st Congress, 1st Sess.

Johnson, B.B. (1981). The Indian Child Welfare Act of 1978: Implications for practice. *Child Welfare, 60*(7), 435-446.

Kadushin, A. & Martin, J.A. (1988). *Child welfare services (4th ed.)*. New York: Macmillan.

Landers, S. (1995, January). Untangling welfare debate's web of myth. *NASW News,* p. 5.

Levitan, S.A. (1990). *Programs in aid of the poor* (6th ed.). Baltimore, MD: Johns Hopkins University Press.

L.J. By and Through Darr v. Massinga, 838 F.2d 118 (4th Cir. 1988), cert. den. 109 S. Ct 816 (1989).

Lyslo, A. (1967). Adoptive placement of American-Indian children with non-Indian families- Part 1. *Child Welfare, 46,* 3-6.

MacEachron, A.E. (1992). *The effectiveness of the Indian Child Welfare Act of 1978: A national analysis.* Tempe, AZ: Unpublished manuscript of the American Indian Projects Office, School of Social Work, Arizona State University.

National Black Child Development Institute. (1989). *Who will care when parents can't?* Washington, DC: Author.

National Center on Child Abuse and Neglect, (1994). *Child maltreatment 1992: Reports from the states to the National Center on Child Abuse and Neglect.* Washington, DC: Author.

National Institute on Drug Abuse. (1989). *Overview of selected drug trends.* Rockville, MD: Author.

Office of Smoking and Health. (1988). *The health consequences of smoking: Nicotine addiction.* Washington, DC: U.S. Government Printing Office.

Pelton, L. (1989). Enabling child welfare agencies to promote family preservation. *Social Work, 38,* 491-493.

Plantz, M., Hubbell, R., Barrett, B., & Dobrec, A. (1989). Indian child welfare: A status report. *Children Today, 18*(10), 24-29.

Proceedings of the conference on the care of dependent children (1909, January 25-26). (60th Congress, 2nd Sess., Doc. No. 721). Washington, DC: U.S. Government Printing Office.

Prucha, F.P. (1985). *The Indians in American Society: From the revolutionary war to the present.* Berkeley, CA: University of California Press.

Prucha, F.P. (Ed.). (1990). *Documents of the United States Indian policy.* Lincoln, NE: University of Nebraska Press.

Pumphrey, R.E. & Pumphrey, M.W. (Eds.). (1961). *The heritage of American social work.* New York: Columbia.

Reddy, M.A. (1993). *Statistical record of Native North Americans.* Detroit, MI: Gale Research, Inc.

Rosengren, J. (1990). Alcohol: A bigger drug problem? *Minnesota Medicine, 73,* 33-34.

Scope of the problem. (1974, Winter). *Indian Family Defense.*

Select Committee on Children, Youth & Families. (1989) *Born hooked: Confronting the impact of perinatal substance abuse.* Washington, DC: U.S. Government Printing Office.

Streissguth, A., Sampson, P., & Barr, H. (1989). Neurobehavioral dose-response effects of prenatal alcohol exposure in humans from infancy to adulthood. In D.E. Hutchings (Ed.), *Prenatal abuse of licit and illicit drugs* (pp. 145-158). New York: New York Academy of Sciences.

Suter v. Artist M., 112 S. Ct. 1360 (1992).

Tartara, T. (1988). *Characteristics of children in substitute care: A statistical summary of the VCIS national child welfare data base.* Washington, DC: American Public Welfare Association.

Thurston, H.W. (1930). *The dependent child.* New York: Columbia University Press.

U.S. Department of Health and Human Services. (1988) *Study findings: Study of national incidence and prevalence of child abuse and neglect.* Washington, DC: U.S. Government Printing Office.

U.S. Department of Justice. (1994). *Prisoners in 1993.* Bureau of Justice Statistics, Office of Justice Programs, Washington, DC: Author.

U.S. General Accounting Office. (1993). *Foster care: Services to prevent out-of-home placements are limited by funding barriers (GAO/HRD-93-76).* Washington, DC: U.S.Government Printing Office.

U.S. General Accounting Office. (1995). *Child welfare: Opportunities to further enhance family preservation and support activities (GAO/HEHS-95-112).* Washington DC: U.S.Government Printing Office.

Zuckerman, B. & Frank D. (1992). Crack kids not broken. *Pediatrics, 89,* 337-339.

Thoughts on Poverty and Inequality

Marcia Widmer

So what is it like to be a single mother? It is like doing a high wire act with no net underneath to catch you when you fall. The fall, of course, is imminent. Women arrive at single motherhood for a variety of reasons: generational poverty, unwed teen pregnancy, divorce, spousal abuse, alcoholism or drug addiction–the list is a long one. Regardless of how we arrive, when we get there it becomes a balancing act unlike any other. We are one parent doing the job of two, typically at or near poverty line income.

LOSING STATUS

Five years ago I was an upper-middle-class housewife comfortably situated in a suburban home. Unlike many of the women of my generation, I had not completed college nor established any kind of career for myself. I thought that raising children and nurturing a family was important work; after all, the women in my family did not attend college or pursue careers, so naturally I settled for the same.

My husband developed an insidious addiction to cocaine. The drug use escalated with his rapid ascendance into yuppiedom, yet destroyed him and our lives at a rate of supersonic speed. I lost my home, medical insurance, credit cards, auto insurance, and nearly lost my car in a six-month period. Along with the fiscal and material assets, I subtly began to

---

Marcia Widmer graduated with Honors from Arizona State University, August 1996.

[Haworth co-indexing entry note]: "Thoughts on Poverty and Inequality." Widmer, Marcia. Co-published simultaneously in *Journal of Poverty* (The Haworth Press, Inc.) Vol. 1, No. 2, 1997, pp. 95-100; and: *Income Security and Public Assistance for Women and Children* (ed: Keith M. Kilty, Virginia E. Richardson, and Elizabeth A. Segal) The Haworth Press, Inc., 1997, pp. 95-100. Single or multiple copies of this article are available for a fee from The Haworth Document Delivery Service [1-800-342-9678, 9:00 a.m. - 5:00 p.m. (EST). E-mail address: getinfo@haworth.com].

95

lose something even more important–my place in my community. My neighbors, who I thought were my friends, could no longer relate to me. They were uncomfortable when they ran into me at the mailbox or the grocery store. What transpired from their expressionless faces was my new reality–I was completely on my own.

I took whatever jobs were available. I worked packing boxes at The Price Club and then as a food server. Eventually, I managed to get myself back to the University to complete an undergraduate degree which, in fact, was the only way to secure a stable future for my children and myself.

Regardless of my efforts, the necessary pieces of my life that held my family together continued to crumble. The doctor who delivered my children did not want me as his patient anymore–my medical insurance had expired. He formally released me as his patient and told me to apply for Medicaid. My children missed regular dentist and pediatrician visits because I had no way to pay for them. They also missed soccer or baseball that year; I couldn't afford the additional expense. I knew where I was heading. I knew that I was falling through the cracks and that all of my worst fears were about to be realized.

After my home was sold, I was left with exactly enough money to pay first and last months' rent and to buy my car back from the loan sharks to whom my husband had hawked it for spending cash. I started my new life at a zero sum.

THE WELFARE OFFICE

My initial thoughts on the welfare office were: as a state, as a country, surely we can do better than this. This particular welfare office was dingy and dirty, swarming with crying babies and toddlers running around the room. Except for the children, everyone in the waiting area looked depressed and lifeless. The people seemed different because they were different–these people were cut off from the American mainstream, the place I just left. The whole experience made my stomach knot up. I did not want to be there and I was angry that I had to be. I walked up to the counter to ask a question, and the woman at the desk snapped, "Take a number and wait." So I did. I waited an hour before anyone would talk to me, and then I filled out some forms and waited another forty-five minutes or so before I could see an eligibility interviewer.

I struck up a conversation with a young woman who was sitting beside me. This was unusual because people waiting in welfare offices do not usually converse with one another. She complained about the wait and the process. She said she would be late for work if they did not call her name soon. But she had to stay because she needed to be reviewed for benefits and would risk losing them if she did not stay. She told me her husband did not work because he was a drug addict and she was trying to get away from him with her three-year-old son but could never save enough money to move out on her own. She was trying to get an additional job, but was worried about not having enough time to spend with her son, and she was unhappy with the daycare center she had to use with her child care assistance. Soon she was called back behind the wall that divided us from them—the eligibility interviewers.

Shortly after that, it was my turn. I was led back to a tiny cubicle and sat down. I started to explain my situation, but was cut off and asked if I had any of the documents on a list the interviewer put in front of me. He said, "I need your last two pay stubs, a class schedule, student financial aid statements, electric bill, rent receipts, social security cards and birth certificates for you and your children, bank statements and proof of any assets that you own." He continued, "I will walk out with you and look at your car; if its value is too high you won't qualify for any benefits." I tried to tell him I had just lost everything. He told me that I should have come in much sooner, that had I applied for benefits while I was still living with my husband who was not supporting the family, I would have been eligible for more. But now that I was receiving student financial aid and loans, which amounted to about $750 per month, I would probably not qualify for child care assistance or any type of cash assistance. However, I might qualify for food stamps and Medicaid for my children, but not for myself unless I were pregnant.

The eligibility worker did not care about the circumstances of my life or how I was planning to get out of the situation that I had arrived at. It did not matter that I was going to school to try and make a better life for myself and my children. In fact, going to college actually worked against me. What mattered was whether the information required by the list would fit into the formula that would grant some financial relief. I said, "Look, I don't want to be here, but I'm not receiving any child support because I can't afford an attorney to petition the court for a support order in the first place. I'm only asking for some help for two years until I can get my feet on the ground, complete my education, and work my way into a better paying job." He just looked at me in a sort of helpless way and said that if I could get that documentation back to him in ten days that he might be able to issue food stamps, and that the children would be taken care of medically. He did walk out with me to look at my car—the one I use to drive my kids and myself to school. The only real asset that I had left from the marriage, the same car I had to buy back from loan sharks, had somehow become the obstacle to receiving public assistance.

Finally, I did receive food stamps in the amount of $250 a month and my children were eligible for the state Medicaid program. Both benefits turned out to be real life savers.

THE GROCERY STORE

The food stamps, although they were a life saver, were a degrading experience. Because I was embarrassed, I would go shopping late at night so that I would not run into anyone I knew or get sneered at by other shoppers in the check-out line. The first time I used them was late one Sunday evening when I knew the store would be empty. It was difficult, but I stumbled through. After I loaded my bags into the car that night, I sat in the driver's seat, put my head down on the steering wheel and cried for awhile. At times like that I would pray or just keep telling myself that this was a temporary situation in my life and that, if I kept working hard, it would not always be this way.

CAR TROUBLE

When you are a single mother living on a limited income, car problems can be enough to make you want to throw in the towel. I have experienced many occasions when the thermostat cap blew off followed by green ooze that started bubbling out of the radiator. I have had broken fuel pumps, burnt out headlights, chronic oil leaks, dead batteries, flat tires, cracked windshields, and one complete and total breakdown. I looked on while the one asset left over from my marriage, the same asset counted against me at the welfare office and the one I had to buy back from the loan sharks, had to be towed away as black smoke was pouring out of the engine.

Most of the single mothers I know have the same special relationship with their automobiles. Those of us who flirt with the poverty line are left with the cars that the rest of society rejects. Our relationships with our cars are often as dysfunctional as our marriages were. It is sort of a love/hate relationship. I would do anything for my car because it is the only one I have, but it is never there for me when I really need it the most. Single mothers simply don't have the extra cash to pay a mechanic's fees. The reality is that we have to borrow the money—from family, friends, a man— whatever it takes because we *need* the car. Without it we can't get to work, school, or take the kids to basketball practice.

HOLDING IT ALL TOGETHER

There is no way to hold it all together without some help. I could not do it. Even when I worked full-time and was not in school, I could not earn enough to pay for my rent, utilities, a phone, gas, or car insurance without the help of food stamps and child care assistance. In fact, I lived without car insurance for three years. My children have medical insurance, but I have lived without it for five years now.

Programs like the school lunch program and help with afterschool care from non-profit organizations really helped me make ends meet. Although I will have to pay back the school loans I took, it was actually less expensive to go to school because I did not need extra before and after school care. I did not have the expense of gas to drive downtown or the wear and tear on my car. I certainly did not need dress clothes for college. I had trouble qualifying for food stamps when I went to school because my financial aid came in one lump sum at the beginning of each semester and consequently I had too much money in the bank, even though that money had to be stretched for sixteen weeks of the semester and then some. I learned to apply for food stamps between financial aid disbursements; it was part of that delicate balancing act.

I found myself constantly planning and planning, budgeting and calculating the cost of everything. If one thing fell out of place, like a $100 repair on the car, I would take a hard fall. I could never pay my electric bill and phone bill in the same month. I had to alternate, leaving one always a month past due.

When I worked and went to school full-time I received full-time criticism from friends and family that I was not spending enough time with my children. When I lived solely on student financial aid, scholarships, and loans which afforded me more time and flexibility with my children's schedules, I was criticized by other students for living off the system. One student asked me, "You mean you do not work, you just live off financial aid?" This is one of those no-win situations that single mothers face all the time. Someone is always quick to cast a stone. I think it is fair to say that single mothers, whether they are on welfare, receiving some kind of assistance, or working but still living on a low income, are subject to criticism in our American culture. We are easy targets.

I could have settled for a seven or eight dollar an hour job and had more time with my boys, but I still would not be able to afford to join the soccer club, send them to summer camp, and rent movies and order pizza when they want friends to sleep over. I clearly would not be in a position to get them the braces that they are both going to need for their teeth, or ever be able to help them attain a college education. I have sacrificed over the past three years while I have completed my degree, but all the options involve sacrifice when you are a single mother. It is like being on a high wire knowing that with every step I could fall and hit the ground hard. But if I do not take a step forward inching toward the other side, then I will be stuck balancing an already impossible act indefinitely.

I am now preparing for graduate school, and after that I will be able to achieve a higher standard of living for my two sons and myself as well as try to do something good for this world.

Index

Page numbers followed by f indicate figures; page numbers followed by t indicate tables.

101

Haworth
DOCUMENT DELIVERY
SERVICE

This valuable service provides a single-article order form for any article from a Haworth journal.

- *Time Saving:* No running around from library to library to find a specific article.
- *Cost Effective:* All costs are kept down to a minimum.
- *Fast Delivery:* Choose from several options, including same-day FAX.
- *No Copyright Hassles:* You will be supplied by the original publisher.
- *Easy Payment:* Choose from several easy payment methods.

Open Accounts Welcome for . . .
- Library Interlibrary Loan Departments
- Library Network/Consortia Wishing to Provide Single-Article Services
- Indexing/Abstracting Services with Single Article Provision Services
- Document Provision Brokers and Freelance Information Service Providers

---

MAIL or *FAX* THIS ENTIRE ORDER FORM TO:

Haworth Document Delivery Service
The Haworth Press, Inc.
10 Alice Street
Binghamton, NY 13904-1580

or FAX: 1-800-895-0582
or CALL: 1-800-342-9678
9am-5pm EST

PLEASE SEND ME PHOTOCOPIES OF THE FOLLOWING SINGLE ARTICLES:

1) Journal Title: _____

Vol/Issue/Year: _____ Starting & Ending Pages: _____

Article Title: _____

_____

2) Journal Title: _____

Vol/Issue/Year: _____ Starting & Ending Pages: _____

Article Title: _____

_____

3) Journal Title: _____

Vol/Issue/Year: _____ Starting & Ending Pages: _____

Article Title: _____

_____

4) Journal Title: _____

Vol/Issue/Year: _____ Starting & Ending Pages: _____

Article Title: _____

_____

(See other side for Costs and Payment Information)

COSTS: Please figure your cost to order quality copies of an article.

1. Set-up charge per article: $8.00
           ($8.00 × number of separate articles)   _____

2. Photocopying charge for each article:
           1-10 pages: $1.00   _____

           11-19 pages: $3.00   _____

           20-29 pages: $5.00   _____

           30+ pages: $2.00/10 pages   _____

3. Flexicover (optional): $2.00/article   _____

4. Postage & Handling: US: $1.00 for the first article/
           $.50 each additional article   _____

           Federal Express: $25.00   _____

           Outside US: $2.00 for first article/
           $.50 each additional article_____

5. Same-day FAX service: $.35 per page   _____

                  GRAND TOTAL: _____

METHOD OF PAYMENT: (please check one)

❑ Check enclosed   ❑ Please ship and bill. PO # _____
        (sorry we can ship and bill to bookstores only! All others must pre-pay)

❑ Charge to my credit card: ❑ Visa; ❑ MasterCard; ❑ Discover;
            ❑ American Express;

Account Number:_____ Expiration date:_____

Signature: ✗_____

Name: _____ Institution: _____

Address: _____

_____

City: _____ State:_____ Zip:_____

Phone Number: _____ FAX Number: _____

MAIL or *FAX* THIS ENTIRE ORDER FORM TO:

Haworth Document Delivery Service | **or FAX:** 1-800-895-0582
The Haworth Press, Inc. | **or CALL:** 1-800-342-9678
10 Alice Street | 9am-5pm EST)
Binghamton, NY 13904-1580

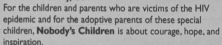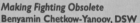